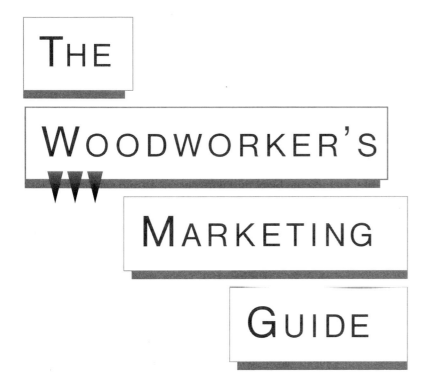

THE
WOODWORKER'S
MARKETING
GUIDE

THE

WOODWORKER'S

MARKETING

GUIDE

MARTIN
EDIC

The Taunton Press

for fellow enthusiasts

First printing: January 1995
Printed in the United States of America

A FINE WOODWORKING Book
FINE WOODWORKING® is a trademark of The Taunton Press, Inc.,
registered in the U.S. Patent and Trademark Office.

The Taunton Press, 63 South Main Street, Box 5506,
Newtown, CT 06470-5506

Library of Congress Cataloging-in-Publication Data

Edic, Martin.
    The woodworker's marketing guide/Martin Edic.
        p.   cm.
    "A Fine woodworking book"—T.p. verso.
    Includes index.
    ISBN 1-56158-091-0
    1. Woodwork—Marketing. I. Title.
    HD9773.A2E34   1995   684'.08'0688—dc20
    94-43972   CIP

ACKNOWLEDGMENTS

Thanks to my wife, Annie Wells, my brother Richard for everything I know about woodworking, John Dodd for the conversations that got me started and Paul Dodd and Peggi Fournier at 4D Advertising who went through the learning process with me. Additional thanks to Helen Albert, Tom McKenna and the staff at The Taunton Press for being a pleasure to work with.

INTRODUCTION

When you decided to become a professional woodworker, you probably didn't immediately think about marketing or sales. It's more likely that you started with some work from a friend or an acquaintance and had to set up a shop, buy tools, find suppliers and deal with many other pressing issues. It was only later, when you didn't have any work, that you became faced with the scary concept of marketing yourself, of going out into the world and asking people to do business with you. Even then, you probably didn't think about marketing; you probably started thinking about things like advertising, business cards and signs. You probably even checked out some ad rates and maybe even tried a local newspaper ad or had a flyer made up at a print shop. And my guess is that the response was so tepid that you may have concluded that these things are too expensive and don't work for a business like woodworking.

Even if your experience doesn't fit that scenario, the fact that you have this book in your hands tells me you need more work, better work and more profitable work. You may be looking for a way to iron out the frustrating feast-or-famine work flow that plagues many woodworkers. Or you may have decided that you need to become more businesslike and professional in your dealings with the public. Whatever your situation, you are now faced with a mysterious process called marketing. Marketing is everything you do to reach out to customers and to convince them that you can provide them with a product or service they need.

I wrote this book to help woodworkers create and implement a marketing plan. As a small-business marketing consultant (and business owner), I know firsthand the fears and misgivings you may have about marketing and sales. My brother Richard has been a reasonably successful professional woodworker for more than 15 years. His shop is in a large industrial building occupied by many small companies, including a half-dozen or more woodshops (the number changes from month to month). He was struggling with the scheduling and work-flow problems faced by most craftspeople, but several years ago we began to work together to solve some of those problems.

Richard and I put together a marketing plan. We made a brochure, did mailings and worked out a schedule of activities to generate a steady stream of referrals from Richard's current and past customers and to reach out to new customers—in his case architects, designers and individuals. We set ground rules: Marketing activities had to continue no matter how busy he got with other work. He learned that sales and marketing are integral parts of a business.

The results were interesting. Once we made a steady, regular effort to tell his customers what he could do for them, work started to come in. The marketing was not mysterious. It was not particularly expensive or time-consuming. Often it offered an opportunity to meet interesting people and share expertise. Sometimes work came in as the result of a referral. Because of his planning, he now knows who his customers are, how many there are and how to reach them. He still has slow times, but they are less frequent and represent an opportunity to work on bids, think about future projects and do more marketing. He knows more work will come his way because of his marketing activities.

My brother's business is a good example of how marketing can help a small woodshop. All of the tactics we used are covered in this book. You won't find a lot of theory here. As a small-business owner, I know you need concrete, real-world help. You'll find a strong emphasis on planning. As a woodworker, you already know how important a plan is to the success of any project. I'll walk you through the process of assembling and using a brochure, a very important marketing tool. I'll also show you many other effective tools you can use to market your business.

I've used the story of an imaginary woodworking business to teach you the marketing concepts in this book. You'll follow two woodworkers as they get started and take the marketing steps necessary to ensure that their new business will thrive. Their fictional experiences are based on the realities of being a professional woodworker.

I recommend you read through the book completely before you start your marketing plan. The concepts I consider essential are covered from different perspectives, and a complete reading will help when you start your planning. Although these marketing concepts have worked for businesses of all kinds, *The Woodworker's Marketing Guide* tailors them to the specific challenges you face as a woodworker.

CONTENTS

WHAT IS MARKETING, AND WHAT CAN IT DO FOR ME?

"What's in it for me?" is the question we ask ourselves when confronted with anything new, whether it's an item for sale, a service being offered or a request for help. For the professional woodworker or anyone considering going pro, it is the question your customers will be asking themselves. Effective, honest marketing answers that question and shows potential customers how you can help them solve problems and fulfill their needs and desires.

Artisans often consider themselves a class apart from merchants and business people. In fact, the successful artisan has always been a successful business person and skilled craftsperson. Even painters and sculptors, such as DaVinci and Michelangelo, spent an inordinate amount of time schmoozing with benefactors and art collectors, raising funds and building reputations that led to larger and more interesting commissions. The wheelwright of the medieval village did his own marketing, hanging a sign that visually represented his craft, going to central markets in larger towns to hawk his wares and providing service after the sale to keep customers satisfied and to bring in new business.

These activities go on today. Business people still use logos that symbolize their expertise. The logos appear on stationery, business cards and brochures. Trade shows and craft fairs display work to potential buyers. Quality service is provided after the sale to create a good reputation and to generate referrals. Those of you who design and build furniture professionally develop relationships with galleries and must bring in commissions and orders through publications, reviews and shows. For a woodworker to be successful, marketing and craftsmanship must go hand in hand.

So what is marketing? Is it advertising, or is it selling? Sales and advertising are components of marketing. Marketing is anything you do to contact prospective customers. It defines those customers, locates them, tells you what their needs are and how best to reach them. Marketing helps you decide what kind of woodworking you will specialize in (if you choose to specialize), what level of quality and craftsmanship you will aspire to and how big you want your business to become. Marketing determines how busy you are now, how busy you will be and how profitable your work will be. It can turn a frustrating scramble for jobs and money into an organized method for generating profitable, interesting woodworking.

▼ ▼ ▼

CHAPTER 1

MARKETING HELPS RECESSION-PROOF YOUR BUSINESS

As a woodworker, you may experience wild fluctuations in the quality and quantity of work you have at any given moment. Going from job to job and bid to bid, you often don't know how busy you will be six months or a year ahead. You might experience a dry spell of two or three months and then suddenly be buried with work you bid on long ago. When you get hit like that, everything seems to have a deadline. It's a cycle of feast and famine, and most woodworkers have been through it. You're affected by recessions, both local and national, seasonal cycles and the success or failure of other businesses that send you work. Well-planned marketing can help even out some of the ebb and flow of work and help prepare for those inevitable crazy spells. Here's how.

Suppose you know there are going to be slow periods, such as between Thanksgiving and Christmas, or during the peak summer months when everyone is on vacation. With a marketing plan, you can use those slow periods to fabricate furnishings for sale to shops or galleries, or you can plan your next mailing or update your portfolio. You could even plan to reorganize your shop, knowing that this slow period is only temporary and that your marketing plan will ensure that things will pick up soon.

So what about those insane periods when you can't seem to get ahead, and people are looking for their new kitchen cabinets or boardroom suite? A marketing plan can help you be realistic about your capabilities and about deadlines. Even more important, good marketing will get you more interesting and profitable work, allowing you to avoid some of those desperation jobs you took just to pay the bills—the ones that always create the biggest hassles and the smallest paychecks.

▼▼▼

PROFIT AND CASH FLOW

When you're desperate, two of the first things to go out the window are profit and cash flow. Understanding these concepts is important because a marketing plan determines whether you'll have either of them.

PROFIT

We live in a capitalist society, where incentive drives the economy. We work for rewards. As a woodworker, you are the owner and operator of a small business. One incentive for a business owner is profit. Interestingly enough, profit is often not the primary incentive for going into business. Most of you are woodworkers because you like to create beautiful, functional things. The fact that someone might pay you to pursue your craft seems almost miraculous at first. Gradually, as you build your business and take on more financial responsibilities—buying tools, paying rent, etc.—the money you receive takes on a greater significance. At this point you may decide that you've somehow lost track of your craft because money is too big a part of it. The money has become a hassle instead of an incentive.

Money is a representation of energy. You perform a task for someone, and you are rewarded for expending your energy. As a woodworker, you can perform that task better and more efficiently than someone else, so you can command a premium price for your efforts. Your profit is a reward for being skilled, and as such, it should be seen in a positive light. Profit is not salary or the hourly wage you pay yourself. It is a sum added to your estimates as an incentive and a premium. Profit may be used to build up your business by buying tools or doing more marketing, or as security against slow periods or unexpected setbacks. Good marketing can help you build in a bigger profit margin by stressing the quality and services you provide. (In Chapter 3, I'll show how to increase your profit margin through your business identity.)

CASH FLOW

Cash flow is the steady stream of money coming into a business. It is what pays the bills, including salaries. A business can have cash flow without making a profit. In a large business, cash flow may be the primary objective because the company has many employees and shareholders to keep happy. For your small woodshop, cash flow is essential for the survival of the business. A steady cash flow is helped by consistent marketing and by developing new skills or salable items that can bring in money during slow times. Planning will ensure that you have the cash flow you may need later (in Chapter 2, I'll show you how to plan your business).

USING COMPETITION TO ADVANTAGE

Your competitors are probably not out to get you. In fact, they are potential allies because you know and share many common interests and challenges. Effective marketing helps identify the things you do best and seeks markets for those skills. A competitor may have slightly different skills and interests. In woodworking, this may translate to different tools, different skills and different sets of priorities. For example, my brother Richard is a woodworker whose shop is located in a large industrial building that was converted into numerous lofts. Many small businesses are tenants, including seven woodworking businesses, three of which share a floor with Richard's business. Although they are all woodworking businesses, each has a specialty. Richard is a cabinetmaker who does a lot of commercial and residential cabinetry. He also builds furniture prototypes for designers. Down the hall is a wood carver who does sculpture, carnival animals and the occasional piece of furniture. At the end of the hall, a grad student builds corporate furnishings, including conference tables and desks. One of his specialties is veneering. Finally, a solitary craftsman works in a tiny shop by the stairs, designing and building delicate chairs and tables.

Each competitor crosses over into another's territory from time to time. However, it is not uncommon for one of these businesses to hire another as a subcontractor, For example, my brother may use his custom finishing skills and equipment to do a job for one of the other businesses. One woodworker may have a veneer press or a shaper and may be willing to turn out moldings or lay veneer as a subcontractor. The chair builder might refer a request for kitchen cabinets to Richard or ask the wood carver to do some work. While life seldom provides situations as accommodating as these, there are lessons to be learned from a marketing standpoint. Know your strengths and weaknesses (we'll take a close look at them in Chapter 5). Strengths are not only what you do well but also what will make you more money. Specializing in your strengths may allow you to get subcontracting work from your competition.

Weaknesses, or areas you are not interested in, also represent opportunities. If a competitor is set up to spray lacquer, and you are not, sub your finishing to him and mark it up, adding on profit for yourself. The competitor's ability to provide that service cheaper comes from his expertise and equipment. You can keep the sprayer busy while giving yourself time to focus on your strengths.

Marketing helps keep your eyes open for opportunities to learn and to profit. Competition is such an opportunity if you choose to look at it that way. By viewing the competition as the enemy, you may be cutting off potential sources of work and profitable resources.

▼▼▼ ELIMINATING PRICE COMPETITION

Effective marketing, particularly good sales skills, can help you eliminate price as a primary consideration when you compete for bids with other woodworkers. Price is only one consideration when a buyer picks a bid; others include your ability to complete the job on schedule, the quality of your work, your reputation, installation ability and reliability. Your marketing activities can help establish your expertise in the customer's mind before the bid is opened. This predisposes them to consider your prices favorably, even if it is not the lowball figure. (I'll take a closer look at quotes and estimates, from a marketing viewpoint, in Chapter 18.)

▼▼▼ EARNING A GOOD LIVING AS A WOODWORKER

Most woodworkers want to do interesting work. After building a zillion kitchen cabinets, the idea of being commissioned to design and build a piece of fine furniture is very alluring. You can use marketing tools to change the type of work you are doing and to raise the prices you are getting for it. By using tools such as promotional materials and targeted mailings, you can create a reputation of expertise and zero in on potential customers who have the money to pay for your expertise.

Perhaps you fabricated a sculpture designed by an artist for a local corporate headquarters, and you really enjoyed the work. How would you find similar work? A simple campaign dedicated to that goal might include photographing the sculpture you built and making color postcards that describe your services. Then you might mail that postcard to the readers of Sculpture Magazine. There are 22,000 subscribers to the magazine, so you may want to see if its subscriber list can be narrowed down to pros who use wood components in their work, or to sculptors who hire out their fabrications. You might consider running an ad in the magazine. A highly targeted campaign aimed at achieving a specific goal and carried out consistently over a period of time can establish you and generate plenty of work. (In Chapter 3, I'll show how you can define your interests as part of the planning process.)

Many professional woodworkers have to struggle to survive. A woodworker who's just starting out or considering becoming a professional often has no idea how to get customers. Most of your time is spent learning the craft, and then, when a big job comes along, you drop your marketing plan (if you have one) and plunge into the work. When the job's over, you're back to square one. By learning and applying some effective marketing skills, you can avoid the cycle of feast and famine, evening out the ups and downs that are part of being a custom woodworker.

The things I've covered in this chapter are my unabashed attempt to sell you on the value of marketing your woodworking skills. I've tried to show the benefits of using even a few of the tools in the book. Planning, ads, publicity, networking, sales skills and the rest are all things that will affect the day-to-day quality of your work. Nothing says you must learn about all of them at once, or ever. In fact, I recommend that you read the book, then go back and do some of the exercises in the chapters on planning and goal-setting. Look at the things you learn about yourself and make a simple plan, using a few of the marketing tools discussed in this book, and apply it gradually over the next few months. Be patient and hang in there, no matter how frustrated you get. Even if you spend 15 minutes each workday on marketing-related activities, you'll have put in about 62 hours marketing yourself by year's end. These hours will pay you more than almost any other activity. You have little to lose, and you may gain a great life doing what you love: woodworking.

▼ ▼ ▼

Leveraging your time

Elements of a basic marketing plan

PLANNING YOUR BUSINESS

Plan your work, and work your plan. Planning saves time, eliminates many errors of inexperience and turns skilled people into experts. As a business person, you should have two plans: a business plan and a marketing plan. In this book, I'll take a close look at what a marketing plan is and how to put one together. The plan you create can be as simple or as complex as you want it to be. However, when you first write a marketing plan, it is best to err on the side of simplicity. This book is full of tools, concepts and ideas for bringing in business. The secret to effective marketing, particularly for those who are new to it, is to pick a few marketing tools and use them methodically over time. A simple plan can make it possible to see clearly how best to use your marketing tools.

The plan I've assembled in the next few chapters is based on a hypothetical woodworking business started by two struggling woodworkers. I'll introduce Arcadia Woodworks later in this chapter, and throughout the book you'll see how its marketing plan evolved. You'll also see how the partners implemented the plan, mistakes, successes and all. But first, let's take a closer look at what constitutes an effective marketing plan for your woodworking business. The elements that make up the plan are the same, no matter what kind of woodworker you are.

LEVERAGING YOUR TIME

Studies done by time-management consultants show that for every minute we spend planning an activity, we can subtract four to 12 minutes from the time spent actually doing the activity. This kind of savings is often referred to as leverage. It's like making an investment that pays a very large return. Time is money, and it has a value in the context of your life. When we use phrases like "quality time," we are referring to the time spent doing those things we savor most. As a woodworker, your quality time may be the time spent completing projects, working on an aspect of a job you savor most or simply being alone in the shop, taking care of business. No matter what your priorities are, planning gives you more quality time.

Another important aspect of planning is that it allows you to take advantage of the power of synergy in marketing, which is the technique of combining two or more marketing tools to reach a specific goal. Using several marketing tools together makes your marketing more effective than using just one or two. Each tactic strengthens the other. A mailing combined with an ad and an article about your unique clock designs, all appearing around the same time, boost your image and reassure potential customers that you are a recognized professional. Those same three tools (direct mail, advertising and publicity) used individually would not have the same power to reach potential customers as using them collectively would.

Planning helps you focus on what you want to do and on those activities that are most affordable and effective. You will be able to to schedule jobs and budget for them, allowing you to put the money and time required aside for the future.

For most woodworkers, a marketing plan need not be complex and expensive. You can handle only so much business, and you really need only a small number of customers to become profitable. A simple plan will help you reach the best prospective customers for the kind of work you want to do. It will also keep you from letting your marketing efforts languish when you're busy with other projects.

ELEMENTS OF A
BASIC MARKETING PLAN

Have you ever taken on a project where the design was vague, and you had to guess what the customer wanted? Would you build a complex audio-visual cabinet without doing a few drawings to see what kind of construction problems you might face? Some of you might have started out trying to build in your heads, but you waste a lot of time and energy when you work without a plan. It's like going on a long road trip without a map. You may get there eventually, but you'll spend extra time, miss many interesting opportunities and spend a lot more money on gas, food and lodging. A marketing plan is your road map and blueprint for future business success. A simple, clear plan will yield great results over time. A basic marketing plan has the following elements:

▶ **An evaluation of strengths and weaknesses**

Your skills are the products and the services you sell in the marketplace. Evaluating those skills from a marketing viewpoint can help you sell your strengths and improve your weaknesses. Weaknesses represent opportunities for future growth both as an artisan and as a person.

▶ **Your identity in the marketplace**

Your business name, reputation, logo, stationery, business cards, etc., all constitute that vital first impression you make with a potential customer. Your marketing plan may include ways to make these components of your identity more effective.

▶ **Customer profiles**

Who are your present and potential customers? Where are they found? What problems can you solve for them? How can you reach them? When do you need to go in new directions or seek customers in new places? The answers to those questions will give you an excellent profile of your best customers, which will help you target your marketing efforts.

▶ **Strategy**

Your marketing strategy is the overall plan you will use to reach your targeted customers and to show them how you can solve their problems and fulfill their needs. It will be a simple combination of marketing tools tailored to your budget, time constraints and personal style.

► Tactics

Tactics are the marketing tools used to implement your strategy. These include but are not limited to advertising, brochures, publicity, networking, personal sales and direct mail. You'll focus on a few, gradually adding or deleting tactics as your comfort level changes or as the market proves that one is more successful than another. The wide range of tools available gives you the flexibility to adapt to changing conditions.

► Calendar

A simple action calendar is invaluable in keeping your marketing efforts consistent over time. Consistency is the secret of effective marketing. By giving yourself preplanned tasks each day, you spread out the effort and expense and reap the rewards of a marketing plan.

► Budget

If all of this seems far beyond your meager resources, take heart. Many of the tactics can be implemented at little or no cost. Others cost money but bring in many more dollars to your business than they cost. A simple budget will help you plan exactly how much you can afford to spend and when. It also will make sure you are getting the most bang for your buck.

► Goals

Articulating goals for yourself and your business is essential for determining the direction of your marketing. A good marketing plan will lay the groundwork for future goals. For example, you may change the nature of your business, such as going from contract work to commissions or building your business into something you can sell when you are ready to retire. Or you may expand your company by adding new products or services. Perhaps you want to downsize and work part-time while pursuing other interests. Whatever your goals, a simple plan can show you how to take the first steps toward realizing them.

Considering all of these elements at once may be enough to stop many of you from continuing with the planning process. I've broken these elements down in the next few chapters to help you learn more about who you are as a woodworker, where you are going and where you'd like to end up. The planning process should be viewed as interesting in and of itself. It gives you an opportunity to find out what you can do to speed up personal growth and productivity, resulting in increased energy and enjoyment. A well-thought-out and implemented plan can get you better work, doing the kinds of things you want to do.

THE ROOTS
OF ARCADIA
WOODWORKS

▼ ▼ ▼

Throughout this book, you'll be looking over the shoulders of the owners of a hypothetical woodworking company, Arcadia Woodworks. You'll watch them struggle with a lot of new concepts and face some personal prejudices and fears. Their experiences are all rooted in reality, and I think many of you will recognize some of your own experiences in theirs. I took this approach because most of us learn by example, understanding seemingly abstract concepts like marketing in a real-world setting, warts, sawdust and all.

Max Gert had a problem. He saw a sign. Not a mystical sign; a For Rent sign, and it was on a building he considered the perfect space for his woodworking business. The building had a dock, a small office, high ceilings, three-phase electric and plenty of natural light. It was in an industrial zone, so noise wouldn't be a problem, and the area was not bad.

Perfect. Unfortunately, the building was too large for him at 3,000 sq. ft., and the rent was too high for him to handle alone.

Max's woodworking business had had its ups and downs over the three years he had been on his own. When he was studying woodworking in technical school, he had imagined surviving on a steady stream of corporate commissions while designing his own fine furniture for galleries and wealthy individuals. The reality seemed to be that his professors got the corporate commissions while he was spending most of his time doing the occasional kitchen and a lot of odd jobs. Because he had worked out of his garage and had low overhead, he had survived—but just barely. He had to make a choice: Either bail out and go to work for someone else or find a way to upgrade his business. The building for rent looked a lot like his dream shop.

Chris Zyslinski was in a similar situation; in fact, he and Max commiserated over coffee one morning after they had run into each other at the lumberyard. They had met in a wood-finishing class and crossed paths professionally here and there. Chris' background had been finish carpentry, and he made the jump to woodworking when people began asking him to build cabinets and libraries. For a few years he'd gotten jobs by word of mouth, taking occasional carpentry work to pay the bills. When Max told him about the building, they decided to give the owner a call and go through the place.

The building was everything Max and Chris had hoped for, a little messy but full of potential. Each was faced with the prospect of taking on a partner or possibly sharing the space. The landlord wanted a real business for a tenant. Max and Chris had to decide if they should become business partners.

As Max and Chris compared notes, they got excited. They had some mutual interests and shared similar problems. They each had a small amount of cash set aside, and each had some tools the other didn't have. However, the idea of a partnership with someone they didn't know that well was a little daunting. And they really didn't know much about business, either. Max suggested they talk to a friend who was a marketing consultant (me).

When I met Max and Chris, they were both enthusiastic and nervous about the possibilities and problems of plunging into a partnership. They told me about the building and how it could change their woodworking businesses. I asked them what form their company might take and if they had thought about names, licenses and especially where their first customers would come from. I said they could get good advice about the mechanics of setting up a business from books. I gave them a few titles to check out at the library. I also recommended that they sit down with a lawyer and/or accountant to go over a few details.

As a marketing consultant, it is unusual to work with business owners so early in the process. I told Max and Chris that they should each do a little homework and see if they still thought they could work together. If everybody seemed to be in sync, we'd start the planning process and work on an image for their partnership. To get things rolling, I said we should sit down and carefully outline some of their goals, take a look at their skills and resources and pick a company name.

Max and Chris were in an ideal situation from a marketing point of view. They were starting out fresh and had a lot of enthusiasm. In fact, reality had not yet set in, and they hadn't even begun to discuss money issues. As most of us know, ideal situations seldom occur in the real world. You may be facing an immediate need for work to pay bills or may be buried in work while waiting to get paid for things you completed months ago. Finding the time to indulge in a "luxury" like market planning may seem unrealistic. If you can spend a half hour a day for the next two weeks answering some of questions in the next few chapters and writing down those answers, you'll understand why I'm so zealous about planning. You'll find out some startling things about your business and yourself if your evaluation is honest. There is no reason to be dishonest; after all, you may be the only one to see what you write. If you have employees or partners, I urge you to involve them in a discussion of the directions you want to take with your woodworking business.

GETTING STARTED

If you think back to when you began your woodworking business, or if you are just starting out, you'll most likely remember getting that first job from a friend or a relative and scrambling to get your shop in order. You were probably thinking of tools and how much to charge, or where to get materials. Maybe the first piece of work was an incentive or an excuse to buy a table saw or a jointer. Of course, you need these things because you're a pro. In fact, a woodworker must put much of his earnings into the shop for the first year he is in business. The basic equipment needed is expensive, and you gradually find out that the hobbyist tools you used as an amateur won't hold up to rigorous daily professional use. You have to spend money to make money.

Buying tools is one of the pleasures of woodworking. Spending money on other aspects of building a business is less enjoyable. Setting up your books with an accountant, having business cards and signs printed and buying office supplies are not exciting. These tedious activities don't seem to have much to do with woodworking. However, the money spent organizing and marketing often turns out to be the best possible use of your dollars when you're getting started. Every dollar spent now on your business is an investment in your future. Every hour you spend planning and implementing your marketing plans will result in many hours of profitable and interesting work. Try to keep these rules in mind when you're writing those checks for printing and postage, ads and design.

Even if you've been in business for years, I'm going to ask you to read and use the information in this chapter as if you were starting out fresh. Step away and try to see your business from the outside. Imagine that you are a consultant who has been asked to evaluate a woodshop that is for sale. Because it is so hard to divorce yourself from your daily work, follow the imaginary business owners in this chapter as they make their startup decisions, then try to apply the process to your own situation.

▼▼▼

NAMING YOUR COMPANY

The first thing to deal with, from a marketing viewpoint (there are other business considerations that may come first), is the name of your business. Names are particularly important to businesses that provide services. Your name is a vital part of that all-important first impression. Some sales experts estimate that first impressions affect as much as 60% of the buyer's decision-making process. This may not seem logical, but you have to remember that we all make decisions based on gut feelings. A goofy name gives a goofy impression, and one is unlikely to entrust such a business with one's hard-earned cash. Unless you make toys or gag gifts, I can't recommend gimmick names like Gepetto's Workshop or Ye Olde Woodcrafter. The latter might be acceptable if you sell crafty gift items exclusively to shows and shops. But for a furniture or cabinet shop, either name is probably too light.

So how do you choose a name? If you work alone and have a name that is easy to pronounce, spell and remember, you might use your own name, along with a descriptive tagline. For example, Jackson Smith, Handcrafted Garden Furniture, is a tagline that is specific and easy to say. Or you might choose a name that evokes a certain image, such as Hardwood Forest Cabinetry, which brings to mind an image of beautiful forests and wood cabinets. Either way, the decision is vital because you are going to invest a lot of time, energy and money in that name over the years you are in business. A well-chosen name will reward that investment; an ill-chosen one will defeat your efforts. For some examples of how to choose a name, let's take a look at Max and Chris, our imaginary woodworking partners.

Max Gert and Chris Zyslinski hadn't defined the scope of their business yet, but they had to come up with a name to file a DBA (Doing Business As) form with their local government so that they could lock up the lease on the building they wanted to rent. Each had been using his own name, but Max always had people calling him Curt, and I had to tell Chris that he was probably losing customers because they couldn't spell his last name, couldn't remember it or were afraid to call and embarrass themselves by mispronouncing it. He wasn't very happy about what I said, but he did admit that his name was misspelled on almost all his mail. That put their first choice, Gert & Zyslinski Woodworkers, into the circular file. They needed to come up with a name that worked better.

A name should not be too generic or sound like a competitor's name. Ideally, a name should increase the value of your business. Familiar brand names, such as Delta, Black & Decker and Coca-Cola, all are worth millions of dollars. For a small business like your own, a good name can mean thousands of dollars in business generated from referrals (for some simple guidelines to finding a name, see the sidebar on the facing page).

Your company name can also add value if you ever decide to sell your business, even though selling it may not be a major consideration when you're starting out. However, the sale of your business should figure into your retirement plans, even if it is only an option. The value of a good name is increased when you don't use your own name in the company name. Buyers choosing between Joseph Block and Sons and The Woodwright Company are faced with the possibility of having to change company names if they purchase Joe Block's business, and Joe doesn't come with it.

If you have a name that fits all the criteria I mentioned before, and you plan to stay around for a while, by all means use your name. The Thos. Moser, Cabinetmaker ads in The New Yorker have been very successful. Thos. Moser is now a large business building fine furnishings in factories. His original ads have spawned so many imitators that I doubt they are effective anymore, but the name is familiar to thousands of people.

YOU'VE GOT A NAME, NOW WHAT?

Max and Chris were excited when we met again. Using the guidelines I had given them, they found a name, Arcadia Woodworks. Arcadia was a pastoral region of ancient Greece. Max and Chris picked up the Woodworks part from a business several hundred miles away and decided to use it because it was easy to say and general enough for their needs. I thought they had done a great job. The name fit all my requirements and easily lent itself to a logo and a tagline once they knew more about the type of business they would pursue.

Arcadia Woodworks is a good name because it is relatively unique and not too specific. Many businesses use the word "arcadia," but few are woodshops, and none of them are located near Max and Chris' town. If Max and Chris were producing products for the national market, I would have suggested that they search for a unique name that could be registered as a trademark to protect them from being ripped off by imitators. However, because they are a small business providing a unique service and because

FINDING AN EFFECTIVE NAME

Here are some tips you can use in your search for a company name. Because the name of your business is important to your success, allow yourself adequate time to come up with a good one.

1. Check out the Yellow Pages under "Woodworkers" to see which names get your attention. Go to the library to use the Yellow Pages from neighboring cities to find more business names. This search will also eliminate names that are similar to other woodwork business names.

2. While you're at the library, make a list of wood- and craft-related names and go through the dictionary, the thesaurus and word-origin books to find synonyms. If word play is not your cup of tea, get a writer or an artist friend to help. Crossword and Scrabble addicts also may be good at this.

3. Look for historical or mythological allusions. Woodworking is an ancient craft, and there are many references to crafts, forests, wood and trees in books at the library.

4. Brainstorm. Brainstorming was developed by advertising people in the late 1940s. Get together with several people, explain the problem you are trying to solve and write down every answer people come up with on a large pad of paper or on a blackboard. There are no rules and no unacceptable answers. Keep going until you have a lot of material or until you run out of steam. Tap into your subconscious. Sometimes your mind is close to a solution, and you just have to listen to other ideas to find it.

5. Assemble a list of 15 to 20 names and try them out on friends or relatives. Say the names out loud and answer the phone with them. Do the names roll off the tongue easily? Are they clear in their meaning?

6. Come up with descriptive taglines and try them with the names (for more on taglines, see p. 18).

developing trademarks can be expensive, I wasn't worried about the name. If you are contemplating creating a unique product line for a bigger market, contact an attorney familiar with trademark law and think about names more seriously.

The one thing that concerned me about Arcadia Woodworks was that it didn't tell a lot about the business. A consumer might think it was a furniture store, a lumberyard or possibly a remodeling business. This vagueness worked both ways. It didn't peg Chris and Max into one type of business, but it could have caused confusion. Fortunately, they coped with this problem easily by adding a descriptive tagline.

A TAGLINE DEFINES YOUR BUSINESS

A brief tagline added to your name can define your business more clearly, highlight a specialty and make you more memorable. Unlike a name, a tagline can be changed easily without undoing the reputation you've built. A general woodworker often gradually works into a certain niche, and these niches often mean the difference between success and failure for a growing business. I'll take a closer look at finding your niche, or strength, in Chapter 5. For now, it is important to remember that you can use your tagline to highlight your specialty area.

Taglines need not be complicated; in fact, the simpler, the better. My brother Richard uses his own name plus a simple tagline: Richard Edic, Custom Cabinetry and Woodworking. The tagline emphasizes the cabinetry aspect of his business without closing the door on other kinds of work. He uses the tagline on his letterhead, business cards and brochures. Other taglines might emphasize specialties like Sculpture Fabrication, Furniture Prototypes for Manufacturers, Wood Carving and Turning, Architectural Woodwork and Custom Moldings, etc. Generic taglines include Cabinetmakers, Professional Woodworking, Commercial and Residential Cabinetry, etc.

Try not to be too specific with your tagline. For instance, if you do a variety of work, be careful that your name and tagline don't pigeonhole you. A company called Monroe Laminated Cabinetry might do all kinds of cabinetry but might be losing customers because its name excludes styles of cabinets other than laminate.

It is also important to consider the type of work you do most often as opposed to what you see yourself doing ideally. I have a friend whose letterhead says Wood Carving and Sculpture but whose bread and butter is furniture. He either needs to reevaluate his skills or remarket himself to customers seeking his carving skills. Again, the skills evaluations in Chapter 5 will help you see your business from your customer's viewpoint and determine whether you have strayed or have simply found a more profitable niche and not realized it. I mention it now because it affects your choice of a business name and tagline. You may decide to add or change a tagline once you've reevaluated your skills.

CREATING AN IDENTITY

Once you have come up with an effective name and tagline, you have two vital components of what is known in marketing circles as your identity, or image. The third component of your identity is a logo or visual symbol of your business. Before I discuss logos, though, I want to clarify some things about identity.

Part of developing a good attitude about marketing is coming to grips with the idea that you and your skills are a commodity that can be packaged and sold to prospective customers. You may think of yourself as an artist who is above the somewhat seedy world of commerce. Yet, as a business person, you are involved in the marketplace all the time, and you are packaged in the eyes of your customers whether you like it or not. They know you as a woodworker first, as a person second. If you place yourself above the dust and dirt of the marketplace, you are relinquishing control over how you are perceived by others. Although you may see yourself as a highly skilled artisan worthy of respect and top prices, your customers may see you simply as a high-priced carpenter. Your marketing, and particularly the decisions you make regarding your name, tagline and logo, can either elevate your status and value or lower it.

Taking an active interest in how you are perceived by others pays direct benefits to you, including higher self-esteem, more profits, better work, fewer hassles and being treated as a skilled professional rather than as a lower form of life. It's your choice. However, I think that a little time and money spent developing a professional image easily improve the quality of your woodworking life.

DEVELOPING A LOGO

A logo is a visual symbol of your business. The key word here is visual. We live in a visually oriented society. In fact, most of us represent thoughts in our minds as pictures, which is not surprising, considering the number of images we are exposed to on television, in newspapers and elsewhere. The average American living in a metropolitan area is exposed to over 1,500 advertisements daily. Visual symbols are easy to remember and can convey a lot of information instantly.

Logos are a proud tradition among craftspeople. One reason is because long ago many of their customers could not read. Signs always carried a symbol of the craft so that illiterate customers would know what kind of business they were walking into. Illiteracy is less of a concern today, but as a woodworker, you're creating pieces consisting of visually pleasing shapes and textures. Many of your prospective customers may be unusually visually literate, such as architects, interior designers, gallery owners and art collectors. Appealing to the visual sense of your customers is vital, and it starts with a logo.

Choosing or creating a logo may mean contacting a professional graphic designer with experience in this area. I do not recommend having an artistic friend design a logo unless he or she is skilled at this kind of design and understands the marketing ideas behind logos. Homemade logos tend to be overly complicated, poorly rendered or amateurish, which reflect poorly upon you. Developing a relationship with a good designer at this stage can mean that your logo will be professional and easy to look at. It will convey a straight-ahead message and will be consistent from business card to brochure to postcard. In Chapter 12, I discuss in detail the process of working with a designer.

Logos can be expensive, ranging from $250 to $2,000 and up for a custom-designed one. Often a logo is a worthwhile investment, and you may be able to trade work for design services. If you can't afford to spend a lot of money, you can have a designer set your name and tagline in a decorative typeface, creating a logo composed entirely of type. When well done, this can be very effective and serves many businesses more than adequately. Then you can take existing art (often known as clip art) that is in the public domain (copyright free) and have your designer add your type logo to it. Many books and computer disks of clip art are available, containing thousands of images from which to choose. Often a designer will take an image and silhouette or alter it to make it unique. My brother's designer found an old German woodcut of a plane surrounded by shavings in a decorative pattern and used it as-is for a logo. It has drawn many compliments, particularly from the architects and the designers he works with.

If you opt for a custom logo, your designer should understand your business and be aware of your marketing plans and ideas. Then the designer will come up with a number of sketches for you to choose from. Keep in mind the same criteria used in choosing a name: simplicity, a clear message and an easily remembered image. The graphic should say something about your business. Too many logos consist of an abstract piece of art that tells nothing about you and your work. Why miss this opportunity to reinforce your message? Having said this, I should add that it is important that you don't try to say too much with a logo. The kitchen-sink approach just looks indecisive and low budget.

So what about Arcadia Woodworks? The tagline was easy: Fine Woodworking and Cabinetry. Chris was ready with that one because he'd been using it for years. The tagline had the added benefit of giving him some continuity with his previous business, important in light of all the big changes he would be going through. And Max knew a graphic designer from school who needed more work for her portfolio and might consider a trade. She had an idea about using clip art of a tree, repeated in a pattern behind the name.

With a name, a logo in the works and a signed lease, Chris and Max were getting ready to plunge into their new shop. However, they had a few weeks until they could occupy the building, and I recommended using some of that time to start planning how and where they were going to find customers for Arcadia Woodworks. The first step was to set goals and to make plans to achieve them.

CHAPTER 4

SETTING GOALS

Becoming a professional woodworker is often your primary goal when you start thinking about going into business. Unfortunately, it is often the only goal that is specific in your mind. The other things you might be working toward are often vague and get lost in the shuffle of day-to-day work. Yet setting specific goals for yourself and your business and regularly revising those goals will do more to increase the quality of your life as a woodworker than almost any other planning activity. Knowing what you want makes it possible to use your marketing efforts to help achieve your goals, no matter what they are.

▼ ▼ ▼

SETTING LONG-TERM GOALS

Your goals can be almost mystical or extremely specific and down to earth. The goals you set for yourself will determine which marketing decisions you will make and which marketing tools you will use. For example, suppose you have advanced to the point where your furniture-making skills and furniture designs are refined enough to be considered fine art or craft. You would like to establish a reputation as a nationally known artist/craftsperson, attracting the commissions and the gallery exposure that such a reputation deserves. You know how difficult it is to achieve such a reputation, but you're determined to try. The problem is knowing where to start. Your goal is set, but you're not sure how to achieve it.

The first step in realizing your goal is understanding what it takes to reach that level and dedicating your life to it. Talk to or read about others who have achieved a similar dream. Read about famous woodworkers, familiarize yourself with their work and, if possible, write to them, asking what kinds of experiences they had. You'll find that they often had a clear vision of their work. The aspect you probably won't hear about is their willingness to market themselves relentlessly at every stage of their careers. This unglamorous and somewhat self-centered "careerism" is part of achieving fame. Is it something you will be comfortable with, even come to enjoy?

Having done some soul-searching and some basic research, you decide that, yes, you like to schmooze with the art world and are willing to get out of the shop and promote yourself a bit. In fact, if it will allow you to reach a certain level as an artist, you'll make the sacrifice. The next step is to write your goals down. Once they are staring you in the face, break them down into steps. The steps for achieving fame and fortune (I can hear you laughing cynically) might include the following:

1. Raise your craft level to beyond superlative.

2. Develop your design skills until they rival those of a fine sculptor.

3. Build enough unique pieces to assemble a stellar portfolio.

4. Build a local and regional reputation through gallery showings, invitational shows, articles by and about you, etc.

5. Get representation by a nationally known gallery based on your local and regional reputation and on your work.

6. Put on a one-man show that garners favorable reviews.

7. Parlay show(s) into books, articles and commissions.

8. Get to know the many art-world insiders who can keep you in the limelight.

9. Sell works for large sums to major museums around the world.

10. Buy 350-acre farm with a state-of-the-art workshop and apprentices at your beck and call.

Obviously, I'm a little tongue-in-cheek here, but a woodworker from my area has achieved all of these things. His success shows that a high-level goal is possible.

A STEP-BY-STEP PLAN

As my example shows, there are several things you need to do when planning your career as a woodworker. First, you must define your goals. Then you must make a plan and implement it.

DEFINE YOUR GOALS

Decide on your long-term goals and write them down. Where would you like to be three or four years from now as a business? What kind of work would you prefer to be doing? Do you want to expand and have employees, or are you happier as a lone wolf? What are your financial needs? What happens when you want to retire or at least cut back a bit? Do you want to build a business you can sell, or will you put something away toward retirement over the years?

Working these things out now helps define your goal and gives you specific targets to aim for. Once you start writing down your dreams, you may find that some of them lose their luster and begin to look a little less desirable. This is a great thing to find out now before you dedicate a portion of your life to achieving something you may not really want. An old expression says, "Be careful what you ask for because you just might get it." Fame may result in seldom actually putting a chisel to wood and more wheeling and dealing, leaving the woodworking to skilled assistants. Having a bustling shop with three or four employees may mean mountains of paperwork and expenses and an endless scramble to generate enough work to cover your overhead. Or it might mean doing large, interesting projects all around the country for major corporations. It's all what you make of it.

MAKE A PLAN, AND MAKE IT WORK

Once you've set your goals, you must make a plan to achieve them. Who you are, what you do, how much you enjoy it and whom you do it with all are important considerations. Take it step by step. Break down your long-term goals into smaller, short-term goals. Planning is an on-going process, and each step will get more and more specific as you go on. Achieving these short-term goals is vital to your long-term success.

If your goal is to start a business building highly functional and beautiful custom kitchens, your steps might include opening a shop, marketing to persons who can afford such kitchens and assembling a design portfolio. These steps in turn will break down into more specific ones, like creating a brochure, contacting designers and buyers, finding resources for parts and hardware, developing special installation and finishing skills or developing relationships with other craftspeople. You might refine your steps into a daily calendar of marketing and organizational activities that bring in work and keep it up to your high standards and allow you to stay within your tight schedule.

Good plans are broken down into increments that you can easily achieve. I remember being mystified by the construction of a dovetailed drawer before I knew anything about woodworking. How could anyone make such precise joints and get everything to fit perfectly; how could the drawer operate so well, be square and not warp or crack? The first time I saw the rough-sawn hardwood lumber my brother has delivered to his shop, I had a hard time picturing those dirty boards becoming a beautiful, functional object. Only after I learned all the steps, from planing to dovetailing to assembly, did I understand how such a thing was made. Now it seems a normal task because I know the steps involved. Setting goals and breaking them down into steps will help you achieve your goals as a woodworker.

So what does this have to do with marketing? Marketing provides many of the tools you will need to achieve your goals. Many of the steps you must define and take involve marketing and promoting yourself and your business. By combining your personal and business goals with your marketing goals, you'll improve the quality and profitability of your woodworking business. Goal-setting also helps define your vision as a woodworker. In fact, at Arcadia Woodworks, Chris and Max's personal goals changed in light of their new partnership and the responsibilities it entailed.

ARCADIA DEFINES ITS BUSINESS GOALS

▼ ▼ ▼

Once Chris and Max had signed a lease, registered a name and written up a partnership agreement, reality set in. Soon they would open their doors as Arcadia Woodworks, and the bills would start coming in. At this point, I felt it was important that they get a marketing plan together to bring work in as soon as possible and to keep it coming. To create a road map for success, they first had to set some specific goals. The key word here is specific.

Naturally, when we started to discuss goals, both Max and Chris were a little vague about what they wanted. Chris said he wanted a fulfilling work situation that didn't involve working for others doing work he didn't like. Max said he didn't want to do simple, mundane work; instead, he saw himself as an artist in wood. Chris said he was an artist, too, but he didn't see why they should restrict themselves to working with wood. If a customer wanted laminated countertops or cabinets, or specified medium-density fiberboard (MDF) as the material for an audio-visual cabinet, he wasn't going to put his nose up. It was work, he said, and it paid the bills. Max started to protest, and I saw the whole discussion heading down a negative path. I stopped them before they made a mountain out of a molehill.

I asked them to write down, in positive statements, where they would like to be a year down the road and three years down the road. I asked them to consider how much money they would like to make and what kind of work they would prefer to do. The results were interesting. Max wanted to show his work in a good local gallery by year's end and eventually to have a one-person show. He needed to take home around $25,000 a year and hoped to focus on both furniture and building prototypes for architects and designers. It was the career path laid out for him by teachers at the fine-arts school he'd attended.

Chris, on the other hand, was a bit more pragmatic. He had worked as a finish carpenter and knew he could go back to trimming out condos and making decent money. But he viewed that option as a worst-case scenario. He got started in woodworking when friends asked him to build a library for them that would match the original white-oak trim in their turn-of-the-century house. He jumped at the chance to do something more creative and didn't look back. The jobs had been coming in slowly, and he had taken a pay cut to become a woodworker, but he was determined to make it work. His one-year goals were to pay the bills, to get more cabinetry work, especially in historic styles, and eventually to make good money; for him that meant $30,000 to $40,000 per year. Over the long run, he would consider hiring employees and taking on bigger architectural jobs. He was hoping the new business partnership would make that possible.

Max and Chris appeared to have incompatible and possibly irreconcilable goals, but it was more a matter of differing experience and backgrounds. I encouraged them to integrate their goals, using one another as resources in their individual quests for satisfaction as woodworkers. Max pointed out that Chris probably didn't have enough fine-furniture work to achieve his income goals at the beginning. Max said he could design cabinetry projects and would provide expertise in some areas Chris wasn't that familiar with, like veneering, joinery and finishing. Chris could offer his experience in dealing with architects and designers, as well as his installation and project-management skills. He also thought he might have a more realistic idea of what was necessary to survive. Both partners agreed that keeping each other aware of their dreams and needs was important.

They decided to focus their business on high-quality, custom cabinetry and corporate furnishings. Their secondary goal was to reach affluent homeowners, especially those who owned older homes. The first step in the plan was to contact architects and designers. Meanwhile, Max would gradually assemble a portfolio of his designs. And Chris even suggested that the partnership might make it possible to build some limited editions of Max's designs for galleries or craft shops.

Goal-setting is valuable because it makes it possible to aim directly at the most-likely consumers for your work. In the case of Arcadia Woodworks, writing out goals may have helped eliminate future communication problems between partners. Most important, doing any kind of goal-setting forces you to think about the big picture. It helps you get away from the daily work mode and get an idea of where you are going. Goals can change; it's the process of achieving them that's most important. You have to learn how changes come about, and then you must try to stay open to them. Effective marketing can only be done if you know all your options, and goal-setting allows you to do that.

Once you have goals and have started to plan the steps necessary to achieve them, you must take a personal and business inventory to see what tools you have. In this case, the tools will be physical ones, like power tools, and mental ones, like skills and experience. In the next chapter, I'll show you how to evaluate your skills and weaknesses. I'll show how you can parlay those skills into a profitable niche woodworking business, one of the most effective ways for a woodworker to succeed.

▼ ▼ ▼

Find a need and fill it

*List your strengths
and weaknesses*

EVALUATING YOUR STRENGTHS AND WEAKNESSES

The more you know about your strengths and weaknesses, the better you'll do at any endeavor. Your strengths are the skills you've developed over the years and should be used to their fullest potential, whether they are physical skills or interpersonal skills. Your skills are the real inventory of your business. By knowing your inventory, you can find customers who need those skills and the solutions they provide.

Your weaknesses also define the level of your success. Knowing them gives you the opportunity to learn and improve and then apply those improvements to your business. This can be hard because it may represent a change in the basic way you do things and may require you to reconsider your priorities. In this chapter I'm going to show you how to evaluate your skills and experience based on the woodworking you've done. This exercise will be particularly valuable if you can ask a friend or fellow business owner to give you some insight into strengths and weaknesses you have developed. I hope you'll get out a pencil and a piece of paper and try it.

FIND A NEED AND FILL IT

Who are you, and what are you good at? How can it help the customer? The answers to these questions will direct your marketing efforts. The answer to the first question will define your strengths and weaknesses and will determine what is salable about them; this is half the marketing equation. The answer to the second question will give you the rest of the equation. Before you math-haters start to keel over, let me explain. There are no numbers involved in this formula. You simply find a need and fill it.

This simple platitude is probably the ultimate formula (or equation) for success. You may ask, if it's that simple, how come all woodworkers don't become successful? The reason is that many woodworkers get it backwards. They start their businesses based on what they know and what they want to do. Unfortunately, while customers may respect you as a woodworker, they are ultimately interested only in their own needs. To be successful, you have two choices:

▶ Tailor your business to the needs of your customers.

▶ Find customers whose needs match your interests.

Either choice works, as long as you keep the needs of your customers first. For instance, you may have built a Victorian birdhouse as a novelty or for yourself and found that you had tapped into a lucrative potential market. So you start a company called The Victorian Birdhouse Company (a great name, by the way). Your customers will be people interested in Victorian architecture, birds and unusual objects. If there were no such people, you would be out of business. In this case, you've matched your interests with a targeted group of customers who share those interests.

Here's a different example. Say you're a woodworker who is interested in professional audio-visual (AV) equipment. As you go through your monthly stack of audiophile magazines, you realize that there are many people who spend large amounts of money on AV equipment. You even discover specialized trade magazines devoted to interior design for AV centers. A light goes on in your head, and you decide to go into the business of building expensive AV cabinetry that is both functional and beautiful. You've tailored your business to a need in the marketplace.

In both examples, the woodworker did not have to compromise personal interests yet made marketing decisions that ensured potential success. Compare these situations to my third example: You've set up shop in your hometown and take out an ad in the Yellow Pages under "Woodworking." You'll do any kind of work, from repairs to the occasional kitchen or library. Once every couple of years, you get a corporate job doing a banquette or a conference table, but these don't come often and seldom lead to more work. You would like more of that kind of work, but you're not sure how to get it, other than the occasional referral. Each year you're unsure how busy you'll be and often blame the economy when things are slow. Your marketing is erratic, and your customers have no idea what kind of work you do. You have a portfolio, but most people go right to the projects they are interested in, even when you try to show the other things you're proud of. Once in a while you enter a juried show and sometimes even win a prize, but nothing much ever comes of it.

This example is a little depressing but will probably be familiar to all woodworkers. In fact, most woodworkers I know have been in a situation similar to that one, which is a primary reason why I wrote this book. The third example is a story of missed opportunities, lack of focus and failure to market oneself. If you're in that rut, you can get out of it. You simply need to evaluate what you're good at and market those strengths; then you must find your weaknesses and decide if they are worth improving. That done, you can start to understand who has problems your strengths can solve; in other words, you can find your optimum potential customers. In Chapter 6, I'll show you how to target potential customers.

▼ ▼ ▼

LIST YOUR STRENGTHS AND WEAKNESSES

The easiest way to understand your strengths is to look at what you've already done. Take out all your files or records or notes or memories of past projects and list them by customer name and project description. The more, the better, and don't leave anything out, no matter how small or forgettable. List all your work for the past two or three years. You may have to go through old calendars, checkbooks and bank records and invoices. If you are new to professional woodworking (doing it for money), list all the projects you've done while learning your skills or pursuing your hobby.

Once the list is as complete as you can make it, rate each project on a scale from one to five. The scale might look something like this:

1. Interesting work, good money, great clients who made many referrals and sent you more work or displayed your work in a highly visible place.

2. Interesting work, profitable, nice clients.

3. Run-of-the-mill job, paid the bills.

4. Did it because you needed the money, never heard from the clients again, no thanks.

5. Rotten work, had to go back over and over again because of change orders, waited months for money, lost your shirt, and the clients were total jerks.

I'm sure you can apply your own levels of hassle to the scale. Once you've rated your work, look at what it tells you. If you have mostly ones and twos, you are on the right track. If you are down into the fours and fives all the time, you should reevaluate your desire to be a woodworker. You don't enjoy the work, and you are attracting problems. If you have a mixture of numbers, you are probably typical. Read on.

WHAT DO THE NUMBERS TELL YOU?

Look at those ones and twos. Are the jobs similar in any ways? Are the customers from a certain educational background or from a particular income group? What about the fours and the fives? Why didn't those jobs work?

Sometimes an exercise like this tells you things about yourself that you don't want to hear. Look for positives. If large, expensive cabinetry projects are your most profitable and hassle-free work, it may mean that you have good organizational abilities, can keep track of complex design situations and work well with other contractors. If you have always fantasized about being a fine furniture maker, this discovery may be disconcerting. Perhaps you would be better suited to work that gets you into the thick of things rather than jobs that keep you alone in the shop for long hours.

Perhaps you'll find that you made more money and got more enjoyment out of wood turning than those commercial jobs you could never refuse because you needed the work. Funny how those bowls you turned out when things were slow are what you remember most two or three years later. It might be time to get more serious about turning bowls and to find profitable outlets for that work.

EVALUATE YOUR SKILLS

The pattern that emerges from listing your strengths and weaknesses may not be obvious. Look for basic skills that are strong and basic skills that need work. These skills are not necessarily confined to woodworking. They include:

▶ **Communication**
Sales, listening, explaining, telephone manner and meeting others comfortably.

▶ **Self-confidence**
Professional attitude, confidence in your abilities and not short-changing yourself in bids.

▶ **Organization**
Scheduling, time management, project management, ordering materials, organizing resources, delegating or subcontracting work when it is more efficient, persistence and the ability to see things through until they are finished.

▶ **Design**
Conceptualizing projects, construction detailing on others' designs, creative thinking and sparking visual and tactile senses in your customers.

▶ **Problem-solving**
Breaking logjams, finding ways around conflicts and negotiating.

▶ **Physical ability**
Carving, installations, joinery, tool use.

These skills and others are all vital to your success as a woodworker. Finding weaknesses gives you the opportunity to work on them. For example, if you dislike selling yourself and your work, you should learn more about the sales process (see Chapter 16). If design is not your forte but creative problem-solving is, you might be particularly suited to working with architects and designers who often rely on woodworkers to fill in the construction details on their designs. If you are extremely organized and good at assembling resources and delegating tasks, you might consider taking on more complex work that requires employees. You might even take a partner with skills that complement yours.

Taking time to evaluate yourself and your business can pay off in many ways. In particular, it can help you understand your strengths and market those strengths, bringing in the kind of work you want. The same evaluation can make it possible to have a very profitable woodworking business, serving a specialized niche. This niche marketing can enable even a tiny business in a remote location to thrive.

MAX AND CHRIS' EVALUATIONS

▼ ▼ ▼

Max was not happy with his evaluation. Not only was his work all over the map, with everything from repairing and refinishing furniture to doing bathroom vanities, but the ones and twos on his list were almost all cabinetry work. And he had gone to school to learn furniture-making! He considered himself an artist rather than a kitchen designer.

Chris, on the other hand, was fairly consistent in the kind of work he'd done successfully. It was a natural transition from fine finish carpentry to the libraries, kitchens and commercial cabinet jobs he built and installed himself. Most of the design work was done by others, with Chris working out the details and contributing to the constant problem-solving that the site work required. He was happy with that kind of work but wanted to expand his skills a little and get into corporate interiors, including conference tables and high-end workstations. Max brightened at the mention of custom-designed conference tables but

noted that he didn't know anyone who actually got that kind of work. He frowned when we talked about installations. He'd lost money on that part of the job too many times.

Max and Chris had had quite different nonwoodworking skills. Max was comfortable dealing with designers and architects; he knew enough to develop a rapport with these potential sources of work. He liked getting on the phone and talking about his work, and he had a well-thought-out portfolio. He was not a great organizer, though, and at installations he always tried to work during odd hours, when electricians, plumbers and carpenters weren't around. His carpentry skills were poor.

Chris, on the other hand, had spent a long time working with other trades. He was also an organizer, who liked to have every aspect of a job planned out before he even made a bid. In fact, he was a little compulsive about it. He was comfortable with people, particularly builders and commercial

architects. He looked enough like a typical "craftsman" that homeowners warmed up to him fairly easily. But selling was something he hated, and he hated salespeople too.

From a marketing point of view, Max and Chris wouldn't have had any problem delegating certain tasks to each other based on their interests and strengths. But I tried to emphasize that they both needed to develop an open mind about marketing and selling their work. As far as their product, it was pretty general, and I thought they should go down to the library and do some customer research to help them decide what to focus on. By specializing in one or two areas in addition to their general woodworking, it would be easier to target specific, motivated and qualified customers. In the next chapter, I'll show you several easy ways to define and target your best potential customers, starting with the evaluation you put together in this chapter.

▼ ▼ ▼

Target your efforts

Defining potential customers

YOUR PROSPECTIVE CUSTOMERS

Knowing your best current and prospective customers is the key to making your marketing work for you. One simple letter aimed at 10 customers could conceivably start in motion an entire year's marketing, assuming the letter says the right thing to the right people. For instance, imagine how easy things would be if you had the addresses and the phone numbers of 10 people who had an immediate need for a piece of custom furniture. Ten phone calls, and you'd be in business, assuming you said the right thing in those calls. Actually, if those 10 customers really had a strong need, even a clumsy sales presentation could result in at least one job. My goal is to help you find potential customers and to develop the tools necessary to get profitable work from a large percentage of them. In this chapter I'm going to show you how to target and reach out to the most suitable customers for your kind of woodworking business.

▼ ▼ ▼

TARGET YOUR EFFORTS

Targeting your marketing efforts is the only way to promote your business without going broke. Most woodworkers don't have the resources to do mass mailings and to take out ads that will reach large numbers of people at random. This kind of marketing is expensive and would probably not result in the kind of work you want. Even if a large, random marketing campaign did work, either you would not earn enough to pay for the marketing, or you might get buried in requests for work that you are unprepared to fulfill. These problems can be solved by aiming your marketing message directly at your most likely prospects.

START WITH A CUSTOMER LIST

The best prospects you have right now are your current and past customers. They already know your work. They are the best possible sources of referrals. You know exactly how to reach them, you know their interests and needs, and you have already established a relationship with them. If your marketing ignores these customers, you are overlooking obvious sources of business.

The evaluation we worked on in Chapter 5 includes a list of all your past customers, good and bad. If it is not complete or if you haven't done it yet, try to finish it. Your customer list (not the most original name) will be the first item in your marketing toolkit. The list makes up the current inventory of your business and is extremely valuable. Even if there are only a few names, they represent the core of your marketing efforts. The first thing you must do is get that list into a useful format.

SIMPLE LIST MANAGEMENT

A computer is the easiest way to maintain a customer list and to keep track of your work. Even the most basic PC can keep a database with information about the people for whom you've done work. If you don't have a computer, I recommend you get one, or ask a friend who has one to help with your list. Computer services also can help you keep records, but nothing beats having instant access to your files at your office. (Incidentally, it is very important to keep a computer away from dust, which means keeping it out of the shop. It's probably a good idea to keep it at home.)

Computers are useful in a number of ways. Most PCs today will run simple CAD software you can use for drawings. A basic contact-list software package can help keep track of customers, print labels and even generate personalized letters. Some software packages include a daily calendar to help you keep track of significant dates, and some can generate invoices and professional-looking proposals and quotes. You can write letters on the computer, save them and revise the letters for use with other customers. You can store an electronic version of your letterhead and print it when you need it. Once you've used a computer, you'll never go back to the typewriter again.

Computer technology is ever-changing, but you should not worry about keeping up with all of the changes. When purchasing computer software or hardware, do some research and buy what you need now, without worrying about the equipment becoming obsolete. These tools can probably do more than you'll ever need and should work well for years to come.

If you don't have a computer, there is a simple way to maintain a customer list. Go to your local copy shop and get blank sheets of mailing-label stock that can be run through a copier. Write or type the names and addresses of your customers on the labels. These are your master sheets. When you need to do a mailing, take these master sheets to the copy shop and have duplicates made on blank mailing labels. Use the duplicates for your mailing and keep the masters, updating them as you gain new customers. This method works fine for a small list but is very limiting if you want to do anything more elaborate as far as record-keeping. But it's a start. Make copies of your list and store them away from the originals. (You should make backups for computer files, too.) Add phone numbers to a copy of the master list and keep it in your planner or by the phone. This list is an irreplaceable asset of your business. It represents money and labor.

Eventually your list will have many names, and you may even list your customers according to categories, such as architects, designers or homeowners. Once you've got a basic list of current and past customers, the next step is to create a profile of your *best* current customers.

YOUR BEST CURRENT CUSTOMERS

The following list most likely describes your best customers:

1. They respect your skills and understand the value of what you do for them.

2. They are knowledgeable or are at least interested in becoming knowledgeable consumers.

3. They have the resources (i.e., money, time and interest) to avail themselves of your skills.

4. They are appreciative and helpful.

5. They are decisive.

6. They send new customers to you and give you good recommendations.

Using this list, try to categorize your current and past customers the same way you categorized the work you've done (see Chapter 5). Run down your list of customers and assign appropriate number ratings from the list to each customer. Then look at the customers who scored the best. What do they have in common? Where do they live? Are they professionals, self-employed, blue collar, artists or engineers? What is their household income? What is their level of education? What interests do they share?

The answers to these questions will give you the demographics of your best customers. Demographics are characteristics of a population in a particular market, such as age, income and educational level. By identifying the demographics of your customers, you develop a picture of a typical best customer. He or she might live in an upscale community, may have graduate-level education, may be interested in art and design, might have a household income of $75,000 to $100,000, might own an old house. As you draw this picture, it is important to realize that it will be a rough sketch at best, unless you have a very large customer list or remarkably similar customers. However, this exercise does show a different way of defining your ideal customer. The profile that emerges represents the kind of people you may want to target with your marketing. By targeting a certain group, you will have eliminated a lot of the randomness of the average marketing effort, thus making your marketing dollars more effective.

Let's say your best customers are from the hypothetical group I just described. These people are relatively easy to reach. You know where they live. You know what interests they share. Perhaps they are all members of the local arts association or regularly attend certain events. You can get lists of regular customers and members from many of these places. Those lists, combined with your knowledge of the geographic area in which they live, help you target your best prospects. In addition, and equally important, these prospects more than likely know each other, offering many opportunities for referrals.

This kind of profiling is useful within your community or geographic area. However, limiting yourself to your hometown may not be the best strategy for getting the kind of work you want. The techniques for defining potential customers are an excellent introduction to the even more powerful things you can do when you decide to specialize and seek customers in a bigger universe.

DEFINING POTENTIAL CUSTOMERS

When you consider your business from a marketing point of view, you'll open up possibilities. You can decide what kind of work you would prefer based on your goals, your strengths and your potential customers. Defining potential customers requires a little imagination and some basic research, but the rewards include doing the kind of work you love and getting paid well for it.

There is a customer out there for almost any type of work, however obscure. The only problem with pursuing really esoteric work is that it's harder to define and target enough people to keep you in business. So if you have a specialty that is really unusual, you might consider finding a related specialty that is more marketable to help you stay profitable as you pursue your odd interest(s). In the next chapter, I'll show you how to choose and develop specialized products or areas of expertise. But first I want to show you how to discover whether a market exists for a specialty you may have or may be considering. I'll show you how to determine the size, profitability and accessibility of that market.

FINDING A MARKET FOR YOUR WORK

Let's say you've built a couple of 19th-century style bars for restaurants in your area. These bars are made of oak or mahogany and have large-scale molding, wide railings, brass ornamentation and many built-ins, including lighting and sinks. The restaurant owner who commissioned your shop to build the first bar had pictures of old bars he admired, but he was unable to locate a manufacturer that still built these classic designs. You jumped into the project and spent a good part of a year researching, building and installing the first bar, and then you got the other job through a referral. You barely made money from the first, did better on the second, and now you've gained enough knowledge and experience to do quite well on the next ones. Maybe you've got a line on an old shaper or resources for large turned parts and hardware that will make the job a lot easier. But by building two of these striking bars in your area, you've tapped out the market locally. You need to determine who might want your expertise, how to reach these people and how to get the best price for your services.

Start with your current customers. Can they make any recommendations? Do they get any restaurant trade magazines or newsletters? Did they work with a restaurant designer when they planned their bars? You'd probably find one or two trade magazines, maybe get a name or two and find out there was an association of restaurant designers and planners. The next step is the library. Check a directory of associations for the designer's group. The directory may reveal useful information about the associations, including the number of members, the phone number and the names of any publications they issue. While you're at the library, check magazine directories for the same information on your trade magazines. By now you're starting to get an idea of how many potential customers are out there. There are a lot of them because we live in a country with 250 million people. If even a few of those people are seeking services like yours, you can be very successful. As the bar builder in this example, you'll probably only need a few jobs a year to prosper.

In fact, the number of potential customers, based on one association list and one trade-magazine subscriber list, is way too large for a small wood-shop to deal with. You've got to narrow your list down even more. So you contact both the association and the trade magazine about list rentals and get the statistics on geographic location or dollar volume for the people and companies on the list. Usually you will be referred to a list broker who handles the mailing lists for the association or the magazine (list brokers and mailing lists are covered in more detail on pp. 66 and 67). A mailing list exists for nearly every kind of interest group. A list can be segmented with other criteria, such as zip code, business size and income.

Let's say you decide to focus on restaurant designers (a small list of 200 to 300) and owners of large restaurants in the Northeast, where your shop is located. You rent the lists and start a campaign to reach and sell to those potential customers. If you have successfully targeted the right group of customers, you'll get requests for bids. Perhaps you've contacted an architectural firm that designs 19th-century interiors for a chain of restaurants throughout the United States. This firm has had difficulty finding contractors to build the elaborate back bars that are a signature element of their restaurant design. By targeting your efforts, you've reached a great prospective customer.

If this sort of sleuthing seems like a lot of work and money, consider this: Spending a few hours a week for two months, perhaps 15 to 20 hours total, planning your work and seeking highly motivated customers can result in a steady stream of profitable, interesting work for your business. Even if it generates only a few jobs, you are looking at a very good return on the time you invested in a little customer research. And you now know more about your customers, making it easier to establish the all-important rapport necessary to build your business and to get steady referrals.

Once you've targeted your potential customers, it's time to take a look at the work you do (your product) and analyze how it solves problems and fulfills the needs of your potential customers. Only by putting yourself in their shoes and adapting your work to their needs will your woodworking business become profitable. The next chapter will look at the products and the services you provide as a woodworker.

ARCADIA WOODWORKS TRIES TO FIND THE PERFECT CUSTOMER

▼ ▼ ▼

One of the easiest ways to target customers is to use what I call the perfect-world scenario. You sit down and brainstorm, describing your perfect customer while ignoring any real-world constraints. Max's perfect customers were wealthy, contemporary-art collectors who would buy and commission pieces, introduce him to others and sponsor gallery exhibitions. Chris wanted to hook up with a few architects and designers who did high-end residential and commercial work, such as libraries and boardrooms for clients who were more concerned with quality and craftsmanship than price. He also wanted to get paid on time and to feel appreciated as a craftsperson.

There's nothing wrong with identifying perfect customers so long as you realize that we don't live in a perfect world. The people Max and Chris described were simply profiles of the type of customers that Arcadia Woodworks wanted to reach. The customer profiles matched the goals that both Max and Chris aspired to, and there was enough overlap between the architects and the connoisseurs that each partner might realize his dreams.

However, when I looked at their lists of past work, I noticed that neither Max nor Chris had actually had much contact with customers who fit their perfect-world descriptions. This did not mean that their perfect customers did not exist. Max and Chris simply had no idea how to find the perfect customers and to introduce themselves and their business. They needed a plan. I decided the first step would be to profile each ideal customer. We started with the wealthy art collectors.

Who are these people? They would be involved in the local gallery scene, possibly serving on various boards for local not-for-profit galleries. We thought they might actually own a gallery in a large city—a bigger city than the one Arcadia called home. They would be educated and would probably own an architecturally significant home in a high-priced area. They would most likely be the owners of a number of pieces done by various artisans. It's very possible that they would own or manage businesses that have the dollars to purchase artwork for their offices.

Where are these people? Max would have to start with gallery owners, magazine articles about various woodworkers (they often will reveal the owners of featured pieces), art organizations and the like. He would enter any and all competitions or significant shows in his part of the country, putting together a portfolio of work that was consistent in its vision, and meeting with gallery owners to show his work. He needed to schmooze with the art crowd at shows and compare notes with other woodworkers. He would also ask his former teachers for letters of introduction to key individuals. A basic publicity campaign would establish his name with various critics and media that feature arts and crafts (for more on generating publicity, see Chapter 19). The important thing was that he establish himself in the world in which his potential benefactors circulate.

Chris' ideal customers were much more accessible but are also targeted by many other marketers. A design professional is inundated with junk mail, telemarketing, requests for appointments and other attempts to influence contracting decisions. Chris would have to compete with all this for attention. His marketing plan would emphasize Arcadia's ability to solve the many problems that the designer's customers face. Chris would stress service, timeliness and installation, as well as the ability to work with a team of other artisans and skilled trades. Chris would have to emphasize solving rather than creating problems, and he would have to hone his sales skills, with particular emphasis on developing referrals. He would seek to build relationships that generate a steady stream of work and referrals.

If Max and Chris' goals and ideal customers seem like an odd match, consider this: Reputation-building (one of Max's marketing objectives) and developing relationships that lead to referrals (Chris' goal) are not only similar challenges, but they also work hand in hand. Architects and designers meet and work with the same people that Max wanted to reach. The work that Arcadia would do for the design crowd could lead to introductions among art people. Max's growing reputation (once he has established one) would help Arcadia stand out when submitting bids and making sales presentations. There was a potential synergy here if Max and Chris could put their heads together and work toward both their goals.

▼ ▼ ▼

Make your customers happy

Your product line

High-quality work generates jobs

"Outsourcing" work

YOUR PRODUCTS, YOUR SERVICES, YOUR SKILLS

Many woodworkers define what they do by what they like, rather than by what the market or customer wants. As a result many woodworkers are unsatisfied, doing a lot of work that doesn't fit their ideals just so that they can pay the rent. I'm always hearing from woodworkers who sheepishly explain that the laminate cabinets they are building are not what they really want to do; it's just work to pay the bills. Unfortunately, it is common to meet woodworkers who turn up their noses at interesting, lucrative work because it uses materials they don't approve of or because it fails to live up to their demanding standards for design or style. Invariably, it is these same people who are struggling. Looking at your work from *your* point of view instead of the customer's is a cardinal no-no when it comes to marketing yourself.

MAKE YOUR CUSTOMERS HAPPY

Your customers will use and enjoy your work on a daily basis. Their desires, needs and wants are important because they must live with the work. If they are happy with you and your work, they will send other customers to you. If they are not happy, they will also tell people about it, damaging your reputation, possibly beyond repair. For this reason, the customer really is always right, even when he or she is wrong.

Does all this mean you must do work you hate just to make a living? The answer is no, as long as you market yourself correctly. By looking at what you do, knowing who has a need for those abilities and adapting your work to those needs, you can make a living doing what you like, unless you insist on making something that no one else wants. Even the most eccentric product has a market, but it may not be worth the effort required to reach it. For the rest of you who are dedicated to making beautiful, functional objects out of wood and related materials, it is important to consider your work in light of who will use it.

YOUR PRODUCT LINE

A product is something that is sold. It could be a service, an object, a specialized skill or the resources you have access to. The more you know about what you do and make, the easier it is to find consumers for it. Your products are the inventory of your woodworking business. Your knowledge of them should be complete and so should your knowledge of why people want to purchase your products.

I'm always amazed when I walk into a business, ask for information about a product that's sold there and get a blank look. I used to run a large record and tape store. The store carried thousands of different items by many artists and composers. When I hired sales clerks, I expected them to develop a strong, working knowledge of many different kinds of music, including many kinds they did not care for. I also expected the clerks to know where to find information for a customer when they didn't know the answer to a question. This thorough knowledge of the merchandise in the store resulted in repeat sales from customers who knew they were speaking to knowledgeable people. It also meant that the store did not have to discount prices to stay in business. This situation is no different from yours as a woodworker. Your number-one product is your ability to solve problems for your customers.

WHAT DO YOUR PRODUCTS OFFER?

Regardless of your product mix, it is important to remember that you are ultimately valued for what you provide to your customers. These benefits include aesthetic pleasure, improved quality of life, entertainment, functions like seating and storage, status and prestige and an improved work environment. Many of them are psychological. Think about your work in terms of what basic needs it fills. Does it satisfy the emotional or functional requirements of the customer? All car salespeople know they are selling a lot more than machines or transportation. They are selling status, youth, power, frugality. (I'll go into the psychological side of your work in more detail in Chapter 11.)

Start by listing your products

To find a product line, you must first list the kinds of work you can do, all the specialized skills you have developed as a woodworker and any special items you make regularly, be they birdhouses, conference tables, Shaker-style furniture or turned bowls. If there are areas you'd like to get into, list those as well. One of the goals of this book is to expand your abilities profitably using your marketing plan. But first you've got to know your product line. I've listed here some good examples of what products a woodworker can sell. It includes the actual products and any special services and special skills. Use it to stimulate ideas for your product line.

► Products of your own design, such as chairs, beds, furnishings and moldings. They are mass-produced, in large or small quantities, to cut the costs of production and to develop a market of repeat buyers who may purchase these items for resale through galleries, craft shops or retail stores.

► One-of-a-kind pieces designed by you. These tend to be the products of fine-arts type woodworkers who may sell their work through one or more galleries.

► One-of-a-kind pieces designed by others for specific projects.

► Prototypes for manufacture. Occasionally you may be asked to build a prototype of a design as a demonstration piece for a designer or furniture manufacturer. Once you've made the right contacts, it is possible to make a living at this kind of work. It requires the discipline to follow another's design and a working knowledge of how mass-produced products are made.

► Custom cabinetry and furnishings for corporate use; your design or others.

► Specialty cabinetry for kitchens, baths, offices and libraries.

► Wood turning, both fine art and commercial.

► Carving.

- Specialty work like distressed finishes, or matching existing finishes to historical precedents, colors, veneers, laminates, metal laminates or work to be painted.

- Toys and children's furnishings.

- Sculpture fabrication.

- Outdoor furniture.

- Complex installations and site work.

- Consulting on historical renovations, furnishings, reproductions, design work and finishes.

- Subcontracting your areas of expertise to others. This might include providing finishing, spraying, veneering, shaping, installation and other services to woodworkers who cannot efficiently offer those services.

- Subcontracting certain aspects of jobs to and from others; taking on overflow or rush jobs from others.

- Acting as contractor and farming out work to resources outside your shop, marking those services up as compensation for your time.

- Developing specializations like churches, outdoor architectural work, expertise in particular styles or time periods.

- Furniture parts, table and chair legs and bedposts.

- Repair work.

- Teaching your skills to others.

FINDING A SPECIALTY AND MAKING IT PROFITABLE

Developing a list like this for your product line may help you define some of the areas where you have noticeable strengths or expertise as a woodworker, allowing you to see areas that you would like to specialize in. Your list also can help you determine whom to market your products and services to. For example, if you have a large spray setup and well-developed finishing expertise, your best potential customers may be other woodshops for whom you can provide a service cheaper than they can do it themselves. This is a great way to expand your resources and develop relationships with related disciplines like metalworking and home building.

Once you've established your expertise and have built a reputation for excellence, cost effectiveness and timeliness, you will generate work as well as referrals that lead to more work. One woodworker I know kept in touch with a friend who studied metalworking in the same technical school. The metalworker specialized in architectural and ornamental jobs and sent a large amount of work to my friend. The metalworker was bidding on jobs that often included a lot of woodworking. In fact, some of the jobs were all woodworking, with custom hardware fabricated by the metalworker. This connection has turned into a major source of interesting work for my friend that pays well and appears regularly in design magazines. When articles prominently feature his work, my friend orders reprints. Then he adds a blurb to the reprints, describing his participation in the project. He includes the reprint in his next mailing as an example of the type of work he can do.

If you are a general woodworker willing to take on a variety of work, it will be difficult to define your market, and it will be harder to charge the high prices a specialist commands. One solution is to develop a marketable specialty as a sideline. Then you can use that work to help support your overhead. I know a wood carver who built a reputation for his handcarved chin rests for violinists. He lives in a city with a large music school and gets referrals from string-instrument shops and makers from a wide area. Inexpensive advertisements in trade magazines would also work for a specialized area like this. Instrument-making itself is one of the most highly specialized areas of woodworking and requires extensive training and long apprenticeships. However, a tiny, specialized area like chin rests offers a lucrative niche to an enterprising woodworker.

A niche can be found in many unusual places. Often an area of expertise comes about because someone asks you to tackle a specific problem and then you start to build your knowledge and experience while doing that job. Word of mouth generates more requests for that kind of work, and suddenly, you are an expert in that area. Word of mouth is a tool that can be generated with a well-planned campaign of publicity, articles, ads in the right places and requests for referrals. I'll show you a number of ways to establish yourself as an expert in Chapter 19.

HIGH-QUALITY WORK GENERATES JOBS

Ultimately, what you provide to your customers is intangible. It includes quality, reliability, trust and comfort. The comfort level you provide as a woodworker will bring about trust in the customer, who will be more likely to use your expertise again or provide referrals. Quality determines customer satisfaction after the job is done. No matter what type of woodworking you do, it is absolutely essential that your work be of the highest possible quality.

Never cut quality to save time or money. It will inevitably cost you more later. When you must cut costs on a bid, start by looking for better and more efficient resources for supplies and subcontracting. Developing resources is important. Pricing expensive items like hardware and laminates in a number of places can mean lowering your costs without sacrificing quality. Some items can really add up. For example, a typical kitchen-cabinet job may require 30 pairs of European hinges, 12 pairs of drawer slides and 42 pulls. If you shop around and compare the prices of local and mail-order vendors, you can save well over $200 without having to use a lower-quality product. You can either pocket this money or use it to make your bids more competitive while maintaining the high-quality "feel" that comes with the best hardware.

"OUTSOURCING" WORK

Outsourcing means subcontracting certain aspects of your work to others who can do it more cost effectively or better than you can. For a small woodworking business, outsourcing may seem as if you're giving work to others that could keep the shop busy. But it's important to realize how outsourcing can help you.

▶ Outsourcing allows you to expand the services you offer without spending money on equipment and additional employees. For instance, if you don't care for laminate work but do a lot of kitchens, you can either bid only on the cabinetry, or you can outsource the laminate work to a shop that specializes in laminates. Then you can use that shop's services to provide a complete package to your customer.

▶ Outsourcing can save you time and money. Those counters you sent out to be laminated should be marked up in price. This is easy to do because a specialized resource like the laminator can do the work less expensively than you would have been able to.

▶ Outsourcing allows you to give work that you find tedious to others who can do it more efficiently. For example, 32mm European cabinets offer small woodworking shops the opportunity to compete with larger shops by outsourcing the cabinet boxes to a factory that will ship virtually any size cabinet box, in a variety of laminate and hardwood veneers, to your shop, ready to assemble or customize. All drawer holes are drilled by the factory, and the 32mm system uses standard European hardware that fits into the holes. Quality is high, and costs are often only a few dollars above the small shop's cost of materials. Doors, trim and any extras you add truly customize the cabinets.

▶ Outsourcing can help when you are extremely busy. Can another shop do the lacquer spraying for you? Do you know somebody with a large veneer press who can take on that aspect of a rush job while you build the other pieces? Time is money, and because the subcontractors have no marketing cost to you, they should give you prices low enough to add to your markup.

▶ Outsourcing allows you to offer many options to your customers. Are you building AV furniture for a customer? Offer to build in power supplies, surge protectors, compact-disk storage, special doors that recede into the cabinets or motorized TV elevators. These special add-ons can become an integral part of your work.

Why should you "give away" work you may be capable of doing in your own shop? It all comes down to what value you put on your time. If you are asked to build a bathroom vanity with laminate interiors, four-panel cherry doors, several drawers with dividers and a laminate top that will hold two sinks, you could do it all. You could order laminate ply for the box, cut it and assemble it, build a substrate for the counter, order your laminate, lay it up yourself and cut the sink holes, build the drawers and build custom dividers, then add your custom doors and drawer fronts. The customer would see the woodwork and appreciate the functional, easy-maintenance interiors. However, not only would you have to invest many hours in the job, but your prices would also probably have to be low to compete with the larger cabinet sources in your area. As a result, that work might pay you only $10 to $12 an hour.

On the other hand, if you ordered the box unassembled and put it together yourself, customizing a few things to conform to the design provided, built your drawers and fronts and outsourced the countertop, including the cutouts, to a local lamination shop, you would still be delivering a well-made custom piece to the customer. However, the box you bought was only about 20% over the material cost of the one you built yourself. Labor was two hours as compared to six when you built it. The counter came in at a low price with two perfectly placed holes. If the cutouts had not been right, it would have been the responsibility of the laminator to correct them. Once assembled, the cabinet would look great and be competitively priced, even after you marked up the outsourced components and charged a good rate for your work.

Developing a good resource bank for outsourcing allows you to offer more products at competitive rates. Obviously you can't outsource parts of your work that require your expertise, nor would you want to. However, you can outsource to avoid some of the busy work, allowing you to put your time and energy to work in more interesting and profitable ways.

Considering your work from a marketing point of view can be disconcerting because it may upset some notions you have about being a woodworker. Nonetheless, I urge you to look at the many ways you can make the things you build and sell better, so you can satisfy the customer and generate steady income. There is nothing wrong with being businesslike, as long as you maintain your values and respect your customer's values. When they diverge, and you are asked to do things that make you uncomfortable, it may be time to say, "No thanks," and go on to the next bid. Where and when that happens is your decision.

A PRODUCT LINE FOR ARCADIA WOODWORKS

▼ ▼ ▼

When I next met Chris and Max at their new shop, they were setting up their tools and putting a coat of paint on the small office in the back. Spread out on the large desk in the corner was a thick pile of blueprints, and on top of that were a few carefully rendered drawings of unusual clocks. These drawings and plans were Arcadia Woodworks' first bid opportunity.

Max called his clock designs the next generation of grandmother clocks. They featured dyed woods, metallic accents and nicely balanced lines. Chris' contribution to the company was the pile of blueprints, which were plans from a local architectural firm

for the corporate library of a large company in a nearby city. The library was complex, featuring built-in cabinetry and shelving, workstations and freestanding furnishings fabricated from ash veneers and a variety of laminates over MDF substrates. To my inexperienced eye, it looked like a very large undertaking for a new business until Chris explained that they were asked to bid only on the workstations and the built-in cabinetry. It was still a substantial amount of work.

Both situations looked good from a marketing point of view. But I thought that development of Max's clock line was a long-term project and that they

should focus on getting the library bid out as soon as possible. Max was concerned that his work would play second fiddle to Chris' commercial aspirations. But he agreed that getting a large job would help Arcadia get off the ground and would build a reputation in the local market. We talked about a few strategies for selling their services to the architectural firm, emphasizing Chris' experience with site work and Max's attention to detail. Chris could ensure that the pieces would be constructed for a relatively effortless installation. Max's experience and educational background would ensure that the quality of work would be up to the standards specified.

Max's clocks presented an interesting marketing challenge. I recommended doing a limited edition of five or six of each design to be sold through a gallery. Once he had completed his first prototype, we would photograph it, do a press release for design and craft magazines, emphasizing the pieces as works of art, and we would approach several galleries statewide that handle woodworking art. The clock series would appeal to galleries because they would have a number of pieces to sell, increasing their commissions, and they could reasonably expect some patrons to subscribe to the entire series. The unusual nature of the work would provide a good angle for a press release, making good coverage likely. Chris agreed to help with the fabrication during his slow periods and when clock orders were imminent. He even suggested that, with Max's designs, Arcadia might become a recognizable name in the arts-and-crafts world, like the famous ateliers of the past.

Product development and skills analysis are very important for any business. When your livelihood centers on your skills, it is vital to know your strengths and to capitalize on them. Sometimes this means taking on projects that you aren't thrilled about so that you can move into areas you are thrilled about. In Chris and Max's case, their attitudes about marketing were changing rapidly as they began to see marketing as a tool that would keep them profitably focused on their dreams. One bid and one set of drawings, however, don't make a business. I told them that they had to sit down and hammer out a basic marketing plan to keep those jobs coming and to promote their line of clocks. Once they had chosen a name, set some goals, looked at their strengths and weaknesses, profiled their customers and decided on some product and service offerings, they would be ready to start telling the world about Arcadia Woodworks.

REACHING YOUR PROSPECTIVE CUSTOMERS

By now you've probably got some new ideas about what you do, who you do it for and what you'd like to accomplish in the long term. It's time to turn this research into a simple marketing plan for reaching your prospects. This plan is the road map you will be following, on a regular basis, for the life of your business. It will change as your experience and goals change or when market conditions change. The plan should be an ongoing, flexible guide rather than something that is written in stone.

To help you create your plan, I'm going to write a plan based on imaginary woodworkers Chris and Max and their fledgling shop, Arcadia Woodworks. I'll explain how you can adapt each element of their planning process to your interests and situation. The goal is to end up with a simple step-by-step guide to the marketing activities you'll be implementing during the next year or so. You should be considering both time and money while keeping your goals in the forefront.

CREATING A PLAN

First you need to ask yourself some basic questions. Where would you like to be a year from now? How much business do you need? What kind of work do you want to be known for? The answers to these questions will determine the goals of your marketing plan. Because you've looked at all of these areas in the previous chapters, the answers should be clearer now. Begin by mapping out your plan:

Step 1. Write down your goals. Keep them brief and to the point.

Step 2. Write down your strategy.

Step 3. Write down the tactics you will use to implement your strategy.

To get some ideas of what to include in your marketing plan, take a look at Arcadia's plan. I've provided some detail in the goals to make it clear how they can be accomplished and why. Remember, your plan should consist of targets to aim for, and it should be flexible.

MARKETING PLAN FOR ARCADIA WOODWORKS

Goals

▶ Help establish the name Arcadia Woodworks with our potential customers. This goal will be accomplished by creating a simple but memorable logo and stationery with a professional appearance, including business cards, letterheads, envelopes and bid forms. We will establish Arcadia Woodworks as a high-quality resource for residential and commercial cabinetry and woodworking. We will also establish the reputations of the owners as craftspeople and artists through gallery shows, publicity and the creation of a unique line of sculptural clocks to be distributed through galleries.

▶ Define our potential customers and use those demographics to generate mailing and contact lists of prospects for our custom woodworking business. These lists may include designers, architects, affluent individuals and business owners. Once we have targeted our most likely prospects, we will use direct mail, including brochures and postcards, to introduce the customers to Arcadia Woodworks and to the services we provide. We will also make personal contact through networking, referrals and phone calls to meet our customers and to set up appointments to show them our portfolio.

- ▶ We will establish relationships with local and regional galleries that specialize in fine arts and crafts.

- ▶ We will spend 10 hours per week on marketing-related activities (one hour per day each). If we become too busy to maintain this schedule, we will hire a marketing student on a part-time basis to take care of mailings and other work not involving personal contact. We will market continuously, regardless of how busy we get, knowing that today's marketing brings in tomorrow's work.

- ▶ Our projected marketing budget will be approximately $3,750 for the next calendar year, with the understanding that we have higher expenses this year because of startup costs involved in design work and basic marketing materials, including brochures and stationery.

- ▶ We want to generate $100,000 in gross sales. Of this, approximately $45,000 will go toward salaries, $45,000 toward overhead and materials and $10,000 profit. Second-year sales should increase by 20% to 30%, and overhead will drop because startup costs will no longer be included.

- ▶ We will make charitable donations in the form of works that can be sold or auctioned by local organizations to raise money. These donations will be used to generate positive publicity.

- ▶ We will ultimately create a strong referral network and build our business through long-term relationships with satisfied customers.

Strategy

- ▶ Our basic strategy is to define our lists of customers and target them through a simple direct-mail campaign. This initial contact will be followed up by personal contact, with the intent to get appointments to present our services and experience. The lists will include local and regional design professionals, including architects, interior designers and building contractors, galleries and affluent individuals. Our primary list will consist of current and past customers.

Tactics

- ▶ Direct mail: We will start our mail campaign with a new business announcement, followed by a brochure and then followed up periodically with color postcards featuring recent work.

- ▶ Personal networking: We will join local associations when possible, subscribe to relevant trade magazines and papers and attend meetings. Whenever possible, we will become personally involved in projects carried out by these groups to develop relationships and to contribute to the community.

▶ Telephone contact: We will establish a regular routine of follow-up calls to persons who have received our mailings, and we will maintain regular personal contact with current and past customers to ensure satisfaction and to generate referrals. The goal of our initial telephone contact(s) is to make appointments to show our work and to start building personal relationships with our customers.

▶ Portfolio presentations: We will assemble a portfolio of our work and seek opportunities to present it to prospects.

▶ Sales training: We will attend a basic sales-training course to learn more about communicating successfully with our customers.

▶ Publicity: We will start a media contact list and send our mailings to names on that list. When we complete or start significant projects or have pieces in gallery exhibits, we will send out simple announcements and make follow-up calls. We will position ourselves as expert resources for any questions regarding woodworking, arts and crafts or small businesses.

▶ Advertising: We will run a small display ad in the Yellow Pages.

▶ Follow-up: We will always follow up requests for bids or information promptly, and we will keep in touch with our customers.

▼ ▼ ▼

THE FIRST YEAR

The goals, strategies and tactics of Arcadia Woodworks may seem like a lot of work, but it is important to remember that they will be implemented gradually over the course of a year. Defining your startup activities and making a calendar of monthly and weekly activities will help you map out and implement your plan.

Your monthly activities will change as various options come and go. An ongoing schedule of activities will get you face to face with potential customers and will maintain communication with the customers you have now. Planning your activities, either on a large wall calendar or in a daily planner, will help you see where you will be and where you are going a month or two from now. Many of the things mentioned in this calendar will be covered in more detail in the next few chapters.

The weekly activities that appear regularly on the monthly calendar are the busy work of marketing and should become part of your routine. They help spread out large tasks, like mailings and personal contact, by breaking them down into a daily or weekly quota or goal. If you get buried in work or simply don't like doing this kind of thing, you should consider hiring someone to do part-time marketing work for you. Even if that person works only six to 10 hours a week, your business will become more efficient. The important thing is that you have a plan that keeps things rolling. Let's take a look at Arcadia's first-year plan and calendar of weekly and monthly activities.

STARTUP ACTIVITIES

▶ Design logo and order stationery and business cards.

▶ Make door and truck signs.

▶ Start compiling current and past customer lists on computer.

▶ Start compiling designer/architect lists (from phone book).

▶ Talk to mailing house about other lists and mailing costs.

▶ Plan and produce a brochure.

▶ Put together two copies of portfolio.

▶ Run Yellow Pages ad (call designer).

▶ Join local design groups.

▶ Join local arts groups.

▶ Send out announcement of Arcadia startup.

June

Meet graphic designer and have stationery printed.

Make notes for brochure copy and meet writer.

Assemble existing photos and determine what needs to be shot. Meet photographer and designer.

Get quotes for brochure production and printing.

Put lists of customers and designers on computer.

Compile local and regional media list.

Make up new business announcement.

Send announcement to media and customers.

Weekly activities.

Note: June has many marketing activities due to the lack of woodworking jobs.

July

Finish brochure, send to printer.

Write cover letter for brochure.

Mail brochures with letters and business cards.

Attend gallery openings.

Start phone follow-up.

Weekly activities.

August

Phone follow-up continues.

Show portfolio.

September

Do additional mailings.

Start planning postcard, pick photo.

Weekly activities.

October

Weekly activities.

Speak at designer luncheon on colored wood finishes.

Start turning notes for speech into article for a trade magazine.

Donate piece to an auction to raise money for charity.

November

Have postcard photos taken and order cards.

Send text of published article to designer/architect list.

Weekly activities.

December

Holiday cards to customers (or we could make a toy or desk accessory instead).

Donate clock to Food Source Gala Arts Sale.

Take clients to lunch.

January

Revise marketing plan, if necessary.

Prepare for a show at a local gallery:

    a. Finish clocks.

    b. Photograph pieces.

    c. Prepare postcard to announce the opening party.

    d. Work with gallery on party, press releases and mailing lists. (Max will probably be too busy for other projects this month.)

Weekly activities.

Mail postcards (see November).

February

Gallery show opens.

Interview marketing helper.

Attend area home builders' meeting.

Reprint brochures.

Place ad in spring remodeling supplement to local paper?

Weekly activities.

March

Too much work; cut back to weekly activities only.

April

See March.

May

Attend designer's show-house opening
(Will we be in it anywhere?).

Weekly activities.

The following schedule of activities represents a regular set of tasks we will be doing daily and weekly.

Daily

Mail five to 10 brochures, cards or letters and articles.

Call three prospects to set appointments.

Check status of all bids and make follow-up calls on outstanding bids.

Call one current and one past customer to check satisfaction, remind them that Arcadia exists and ask for referrals.

Update calendar for meetings, association events and conferences.

Read trade magazines, design magazines and how-to books.

Weekly

Show portfolio at least once.

Take client/customer/prospect or supplier to lunch.

Leave brochures and business cards anywhere possible.

Find new resources for materials, specialized labor and subcontracting.

Update and add names to lists.

GOALS FOR A YEAR OF WEEKLY ACTIVITIES

► Mail 500 promotional pieces.

► Make 150 "cold" calls to prospective customers.

► Make 50 follow-up calls to current and past customers.

► Make 50 presentations or initial meetings.

- ▶ Add 500 names to lists.

- ▶ Distribute 1,000 brochures and business cards.

- ▶ Develop extensive resources.

- ▶ Build strong business relationships with anyone who can send us work.

- ▶ Keep on top of bidding and follow-up.

If these activities seem really ambitious, remember that the plan is incremental. You make only a few calls a day and send a few pieces of mail a week. Arcadia Woodworks has two people to split the workload, so its plan is a little more complex. It is written simply to show the possibilities. You are likely to start out with a basic brochure and a gradual schedule of mailings and calls. By looking at Arcadia's year-end goals of weekly activities, you can see how they add up. In his book, *Growing A Business,* writer and business owner Paul Hawken calls this "the art of the incremental" (see Resources, p. 150). It is the most powerful marketing concept a small business person can learn. Those 50 meetings, if they are approached properly, would probably generate enough work to keep two people busy all year. Personal contact must be the ultimate goal of all your marketing. Customers are much more likely to send work to someone they have talked to or have met than to someone who is only a name on a piece of paper.

▼ ▼ ▼

MONEY AND BUDGETS

I've barely touched on the subject of money and marketing up until now. This omission was intentional because I wanted to show several ways you could work around a low budget by using personal contact and planning. Planning costs nothing, and it is undoubtedly the most cost-effective activity you can pursue to help your woodworking business prosper. Also, creating a detailed marketing plan lets you look at the costs involved and decide whether you can afford it. Let's take a look at Arcadia's budget:

This budget includes both startup costs and weekly activities. Some costs are lower because of trades made with others.

STARTUP COSTS

Design for logo	$250
Stationery (business cards, letterhead, envelopes and bid forms):	
Design	$100
Printing (offset, one color, 1,000 each)	$350
New business announcement (250)	$25
Brochure:	
Writer	$200
Design and film	$350
Photos (traded for labor, materials only)	$100
Printing (1,000 copies, 11x17, one fold to four pages, two color)	$750
Shop sign (built from scrap, one large logo stat)	$30
Magnetic truck signs (two)	$100
Total (startup costs)	$2,255

BUDGET BATTLES

As you can see, the total marketing budget for Arcadia Woodworks (facing page) didn't fit their estimated marketing budget of $3,750 (see p. 54). Like most estimates, some things cost more than expected. Chris and Max discussed areas where they might be able to cut back. Was the Yellow Pages ad really worth the money? Were miscellaneous and entertainment expenses too high?

The important things were the initial startup marketing expenses, which were reasonable, and the fact that the other expenses averaged only $65 per week when spread out over a year. I pointed out to Chris and Max that the value of planning a budget was that they could figure in marketing expenses as part of their overhead and know approximately how much they

OTHER EXPENSES

Postage (for year, 1,000 pieces, average 35¢)	$350
Postcards (2):	
Photos	$100
Design (includes mechanical)	$50
Printing (1,000 total at $95 per 500)	$190
Miscellaneous (copies, gas, supplies)	$500
Entertainment and dues	$750
Yellow Pages ad ($100 per month)	$1,200
Ties (Max makes Chris buy new ones)	$60
Subscriptions to magazines and book purchases	$150
Total (other)	$3,350
Total marketing budget	**$5,605**

would spend yearly. Also, when considered as a percentage of total sales goals, their total marketing budget, including startup, was only about 5%, a reasonable figure.

The payoff would come over time, as their plan set into motion a coordinated campaign to tell potential customers about Arcadia Woodworks. The plan would allow Chris and Max to make thousands of contacts, each one an incremental step toward establishing new customer relationships. Because each relationship should be viewed as the source of more than one job, it is likely that their original marketing plan will generate work for years to come. Remember, each minute of planning you do now will mean four to 12 minutes of time saved while implementing your marketing plans. And your time is your most precious commodity.

BASIC MARKETING TOOLS

One of the first things you may do as a new business is run out and have business cards printed at a local quick-print shop. Many other business owners go further and put together a brochure describing their products or services. After a few days, the printer delivers several boxes containing your printed materials, and you take out a handful of cards or brochures and pass them around to friends and any other "connections" you might have. People's reactions to the material may vary, from a mere glance at the card before they pocket it, to an offer of work. If you've chosen a gimmick, such as wooden business cards, an oddly shaped brochure or fluorescent colors, you may get comments from people about how unusual the piece is. Whatever the reaction, when you get back to the shop and look at those boxes containing hundreds or even thousands of pieces of paper, you may begin to wonder what you're going to do with them. If you're like a lot of business people, you're going to set them aside and let them accumulate a nice coating of dust.

In this chapter I'm going to show you how to use a business card effectively, and I'll also discuss other effective printed pieces that can be done inexpensively, including postcards, brochures, sales letters and simple informational mailings that keep you in touch with your customers on a regular basis. I'll also tell you why these marketing tools are important.

DIRECT MAIL

Direct mail is a great way to sell your services *if* it shows that you can benefit the customer. The key word is benefit. If you can solve a problem for a potential customer or fulfill a need, you can get business. Before you can show your abilities to prospective clients, however, you need to make and maintain contact. The stronger the relationship you build with potential customers, the more likely they are to turn to you when they have a need or a problem. But you can't wait for potential customers to find you; you must make the first move. The most efficient and effective way to make that first move is with a mailing followed by a telephone call (for more on obtaining your mailing lists and on sending out your package, see the sidebar on p. 66).

First, you must target your customers as specifically as possible (see Chapter 6) to be sure that your woodworking services can benefit those customers. Second, send a piece that talks to customers about things they are interested in. For example, if you're targeting a list of designers, emphasize the many ways you can help their business. Talk about your craftsmanship, your ability to get the job done on time, your track record and how they can profit from your services. With designers, profit is very important because they make much of their living by marking up items they sell to clients. If your sales letter emphasizes your ability to provide cost-effective services (low prices), you'll probably get some response from your designer list. Each type of customer is looking for his or her own set of benefits, and sales letters are a good way of customizing the message in your brochure for a specific type of customer.

Fortunately, even the smallest shop has an array of possible marketing tools available to help maintain contact that will build relationships with potential customers. I'll take a look at the kinds of pieces you might mail or hand out, starting with business cards. The next few chapters will go into detail about how to produce these printed tools.

MAILINGS AND LIST RENTALS

Your mailing is like any other marketing task I've discussed. Break it down into steps, find the most efficient way to accomplish each step and pursue it steadily, on a schedule.

You can do a small mailing of under 500 pieces at your kitchen table, licking stamps and sticking on mailing labels printed on a computer or photocopied. Or you can mail a certain number of pieces each day, say, 10 each morning. This method spreads out the tedium and helps you follow up on the best responses as they come in. I recommend this approach, especially if you own a small shop. A large mailing may generate too much business for a small shop to handle, and potential customers may lose interest if you are unable to respond immediately to requests for bids or information.

Larger mailings can be hired out on a variety of levels. A local mail-box business can stamp and label cards or packages, using your lists, for a few cents per piece. The costs will be offset by the time you save, and you may be able to use their bulk-rate permit, allowing you to save significantly on postage. There is a disadvantage to bulk-rate mailings, however; studies show that hand-stamped envelopes are more likely to get opened by people than those that are not.

Mailing houses or services can be found in the Yellow Pages under "Mailing." They range from small mom-and-pop businesses to enormous direct-mail houses that send out millions of pieces per year. Even the smallest mailing house can provide services like laser-printing personalized letters, automatic envelope stuffing, labeling and postage metering, and list rentals. If you'll be doing a large amount of mailing, you should talk to a mailing pro, who will get your message out on time.

Where do you get the lists? If you look in the Yellow Pages of most mid-size to large cities, you'll find a category called "Mailing Lists." Businesses under this heading are national companies that compile mailing lists from a huge variety of sources, including phone books, subscription lists, business associations and professions. These lists are rented by the thousand names and are sent to you on computer disk, on gummed labels or on special labels for high-speed addressing machines called Cheshire labels. The rental cost ranges from $35 to $200 per thousand names, and there is usually a minimum order of 3,000 to 5,000 names.

Each list can be used only once, and it is seeded with decoy names that help the owner find out if you are cheating, which is a criminal offense. Of course, anyone who responds to your mailing subsequently becomes a member of your own list, and you can send a mailing to that person again.

You will also find "List Brokers" in the Yellow Pages. These are companies, both local and national, that will work with you to compile a list tailored to your requirements. The brokers are paid commissions on the rental by the owners of the lists. For a specialized business like a woodshop, a broker could compile and tailor a list to your targeted customers.

Why would you want thousands of names on your list? You might not need that many. But if you can rent a list of 2,800 architects in New York, and you want reach all of the architects in the upstate areas, it would be worthwhile to rent the entire list. Lists can be sorted according to zip codes, income, education, purchasing habits, you

name it. A list sorted to highly motivated potential customers will result in a much higher response rate than a random mailing, saving you money and bringing in the kind of business you want. For a woodworker who wants to build high-end audio-visual (AV) cabinetry, a list broker might start with AV Design magazine subscribers, then narrow the list down to subscribers in the Northeast, then cross-reference it with lists of architects and interior designers and end up with a list of design pros who have shown an interest in AV equipment. Though this list might be expensive to compile, it could generate enough highly profitable business to keep a shop going for a long time.

BUSINESS CARDS

Business cards serve a few basic purposes from a marketing point of view. They tell potential clients how to contact you. Your name and phone number should be at the top of the card because many people file cards in rotary card files or card notebooks for future reference. The common practice of putting your phone number at the bottom of the card often results in it getting hidden in a file.

A business card can tell customers exactly what you do. Some business people carry this idea too far, however, using folds to give themselves a lot of room for tiny copy that is seldom read. An effective way to use your card as a marketing tool is to print your tagline on it (see Chapter 3) to provide a clear, brief and memorable description of your business.

When you hand your card to potential clients, they usually pocket it and find it later, reminding them of your meeting. Giving your card to people is a tried-and-true method of opening up a conversation about your business. As a woodworker, you are lucky because a lot of people are interested in what you do. Just remember to steer conversations about woodworking into areas of possible business. For instance, you might ask potential clients if they've ever had furniture made, bought custom pieces or considered hiring a woodworker. Always ask them to keep you in mind if they know of someone who is looking for a craftsperson.

Exchanging business cards gives you an opportunity to get another person's address. Always add any contacts to one of your lists and send a brochure or follow-up piece immediately, even if it's just a brief note.

A silly, gimmicky, off-color or amateurish business card can damage your business. Because you are a skilled, quality-conscious craftsperson, you should not be handing out a generic-looking card, typeset by a printer, with a little picture of a man with a hammer or a saw. Remember, many people likely to hire you are visually oriented design professionals and highly educated consumers. A rinky-dink or gimmicky card says you are cheap, possibly fly-by night and unreliable, or simply not very conscious of design subtleties. Get a good designer to lay out your cards.

DISTRIBUTING YOUR CARDS

Once you have a good-looking, effective business card, you should hand out all of them as soon as possible. They are very cheap to buy, and there is no reason to hoard them. Make sure you always have a supply of fresh-looking ones with you, no matter where you go. If you carry cards in a pocket, and they get dog-eared, throw them out and get some crisp ones. Again, this sends a subtle message about quality consciousness. How do you get rid of 500 cards every six months? Here are some suggestions:

▶ Every time you meet somebody, give him or her a card. You'll be amazed at how many cards you'll accumulate from others, too.

▶ Attach a card to every piece of mail you send, including bill payments, invoices, bids, letters, personal mail, thank-you notes and catalog orders.

▶ Leave cards anywhere someone might pick them up: at suppliers, at your lawyer's office, at your accountant's office, at doctors' offices, on bulletin boards, at trade shows and at home shows; ditto for brochures.

▶ Give clients you've already completed work for several cards and ask them to pass the cards along to friends and colleagues. If your past customers are satisfied, they more than likely will be happy to make referrals, especially if you give them something to pass on. Send cards to everyone on your lists every six months or so.

▶ Staple a card to every single brochure you have. This way you'll never give out a brochure without an additional, pocketable reminder attached to it.

▶ Use your imagination. Stick a card in every piece of work that goes out of your shop. Look for places to leave a pile of cards. I've heard of craftsmen leaving a few in library books on woodworking and kitchen design, leaving piles inside cabinets at home centers and even throwing them out in handfuls at sporting events (not recommended!). Whatever you do, don't sit on them or any of your marketing materials. Make them work for you right away.

▼▼▼

POSTCARDS

A color postcard is an extremely effective and relatively inexpensive marketing tool for a woodworker. But it will be effective only if it has high-quality photography and typesetting, so make sure it looks good. Postcard mailings are an inexpensive way to get the best shots from your portfolio out in front of your customers. They can be used regularly to remind people of your existence. They are extremely cost effective, and the response is often gratifyingly high. Used with a brochure, a postcard can add signifi-cant "oomph" to your mailings. They are excellent networking tools, serv-ing as conversation starters. Color postcards have many other advantages:

► They almost always get read, or at least looked at, because they are colorful and convenient; they don't have to be opened.

► They can be printed for as little as 20¢ apiece in large quantities (500 or more) by printing companies that specialize in color printing and have presses set up to do large volumes of postcards cheaply. You can find these printers through ads in crafts magazines and business magazines (see Resources, p. 150). The photo is the most expensive part of the job. (In Chapter 11, I'll explain how to get the best shots possible on a limited budget.) For a typical 3x5 color postcard with black-and-white copy on the back, the price ranges from $150 to $350 for 1,000 cards. Just send the printer your photo and camera-ready artwork (your message and logo), and the printer will send you the cards. For extra dollars, you can have up to four images on a card or go to a larger card. There are many options. Some artisans I know have cards done every time they complete a significant commission or piece. The cards are mailed to lists and publications, both local and national, that might be interested in the artist's work.

► As handouts, postcards can't be beat for immediate impact. Leaving stacks of them at home shows or inserting them into other mailings are also possibilities.

► Copy on the back makes a postcard as effective as a large business card or ad. The back can contain contact information and a description of your business. A caption on the back can tell the story of the piece featured on the front.

► If the photos and the work pictured are attractive, they will often get posted at job sites. I know people who have hung postcards of custom kitchens in their kitchen as an incentive to do a remodeling job.

► Postcards make an ideal follow-up mailing to your brochure, combining appeal with a nonthreatening sales message.

► Done in a series, postcards can provide a glimpse of your portfolio, showing the range of your skills and services. They are great for announcing gallery openings and shows.

► Postcards are cheap to reprint and do not age. You can mail them not only to your own lists but also to cover a whole zip-code area or a prosperous neighborhood by renting a list from a mailing-list broker (more on list brokers, see p. 66). If you are building a reputation as an artist craftsperson, your postcard should be mailed to every arts-and-crafts magazine there is. The mailing might result in publication or requests for articles or more pictures, generating more publicity for your business.

SALES LETTERS

A sales letter is a brief letter, on your stationery, that accompanies your brochure or direct-mail package. The letter personalizes your mail package and makes it possible to customize your sales pitch to a specific customer. For instance, if you were mailing to homeowners, you might emphasize your kitchen cabinetry or architectural woodworking skills. A letter to designers might extol your ability to get the job done on time and within budget. A sales letter can highlight work you're proud of, including new techniques or areas you specialize in; it can contain references or update the information in your brochure; and it can supplement your brochure by adding details not included in the brochure.

Writing a sales letter is an art, and there are many arguments for having an experienced copywriter do the job. Whether you use a writer or do it yourself, keep the letter simple. Stress benefits you can provide for your prospective clients and write in a businesslike, professional style while maintaining your personality. Letters get read, particularly when they are not obviously generic. You can write a model and adapt it to specific situations, or you can use a generic letter for each of your lists. Computers are very valuable for this kind of customization. Mailing services also can customize letters for you, if you do large mailings.

If you can't afford to create a brochure, a sales letter can serve the same purpose. Simply write a letter/fact sheet that includes specifics about your business, and send that out. The guidelines in Chapter 10 on making a brochure will also work for a fact sheet. Any attempt to market yourself will be better than none at all. By using the tools in this book, you'll be able to market yourself effectively, even if you have a small budget.

FOLLOW-UP

Maintaining regular contact through mailing, networking, ads and publicity can be daunting. Remember, however, that you are investing in your woodworking business and that your efforts now will pay off in the future. For example, a brochure mailed in January may get filed and forgotten until July, when plans for that new law library become a reality, and the architects or designers need bids. They may remember your brochure and call. If you followed up your mailing by telephoning, showing your portfolio and explaining how you could help on the project, they'll almost certainly call. If you followed up with a postcard or an informative article on contracting out bids for woodworking, you will not only get called, but you might also beat out Cheap Charley, the low-ball bidder, or the senior partner's son-in-law who wants to try his hand at woodworking.

Following up helps keep you in the mind of a customer. In some ways, it's a numbers game, with you trying to maintain a consistent and frequent schedule of contacts with potential customers. If you use your marketing effectively, potential clients will remember you when they have work. If you simply send a brochure and never reach out to them again, you will be forgotten, and your money will have been wasted.

A follow-up piece can be a letter about recent projects, a simple newsletter, a copy of an article about you or about a subject relevant to the reader, or it could be anything else you think might be helpful or interesting to your potential client. The material you send doesn't necessarily have to be relevant to woodworking, either. For example, if you collect duck decoys, and you notice your customer has a few on display, you might clip an article about decoys and send it out with a note on your letterhead, "Just thought you'd be interested." Stick a business card in there, too.

Direct mail does not have to be junk mail. It can be a resource, an informative article, an introduction to a new partner or an opportunity to tell the world about your skills and services. It can help establish and build your reputation and can show the beauty of your work to a wide range of people. It can also serve as a window into the lives of the best customers for your particular woodworking business.

One of the keys to a successful direct-mail campaign is to produce the highest-quality marketing materials possible. In the next chapters, I'll show you how to write, design, photograph and print a brochure that will become a basic marketing tool for your shop. The techniques and the skills you'll learn can be applied to almost any other marketing materials you decide to use. Once you understand the process, you'll be free to come up with your own innovative marketing tactics and strategies.

CHAPTER 10

CREATING AN EFFECTIVE BROCHURE

▼ ▼ ▼

Elements of a brochure

Writing the brochure

The copy questionnaire helps focus your efforts

A brochure that describes your services, products and experience is the marketing equivalent of a chisel or a table saw. It is a basic but valuable tool that can be used in many ways to bring in customers and profits. It can introduce strangers to you and your business; it can serve as a reminder to the client after a meeting; it can establish you as a legitimate resource; and it can update your current and past customers on what you've been doing. The skills involved in putting together a brochure will work equally well for producing other marketing tools, including print ads, press releases, postcards and fact sheets. Your brochure will be a valuable basis for all of your marketing efforts—making sales presentations, showing your portfolio or greeting art lovers at a gallery opening. A consistent message is a vital part of the whole marketing process.

Because a brochure is so important to your marketing efforts, I'm going to spend some time showing you how to put one together, from writing, to graphic design, to the finished piece. This chapter will focus on what may be the hardest part of putting together a brochure: writing your story. But first, let's take a look at the elements of a brochure.

ELEMENTS OF A BROCHURE

A brochure is a printed piece that describes what you do, where you are, how to hire you and who else you've worked with. On its most basic level, it can be a simple list of services, typewritten on letterhead and mailed or passed along to customers. On its most costly level, a brochure can be a glossy, multipage document filled with color images and fancy design. If a brochure features a specific product or service and takes up one sheet of 8½x11 paper, it is called a sell sheet. If multiple products are featured, the brochure begins to resemble a catalog.

I'm going to show you how to assemble a basic capabilities brochure. This type of brochure can range from one sheet of paper folded once in half or twice into thirds to fit a #10 envelope, or it can be a multipage piece. One effective format is a single 11x17 page folded once to create a four-page 8½x11 brochure. This format is easily filed and lends itself to large photographs, an important consideration when marketing a visually attractive product like woodworking. It is also relatively inexpensive to print because it's a standard page size. Other fancier formats include assembling folders full of loose sheets, assembling odd-size folded pieces and assembling pieces with elaborate cutouts and embossing. But these pieces do not generally lend themselves to a business like woodworking. You want to impress your customers with your craft and your attention to detail while maintaining attention to costs. A fancy, expensive brochure may undermine your message while enriching your designer and printer.

COLOR

The least expensive way to do a brochure is one-color printing, which involves just one layer of ink on any paper. A more expensive option is two-color printing, which involves two layers of ink. This option is more expensive, but it will give your brochure more pizzazz. For instance, a skilled designer can use a second color, in conjunction with the paper color, to produce a wide range of shades that really makes details pop on your photos. From two-color printing, the next step is usually a four-color process that gives us what we see as "full color." Most full-color printing is done by printers that specialize in four-color work. Although this is the most expensive option, your work will be seen in its best light in a four-color brochure. Your designer can help you make the decision and give you an idea of the costs involved. The designer will get printing bids, which will save you time and money.

Other printing considerations include paper stock, various finishes applied over the printing to create gloss or heft, and various folds and stitching (staples) for multiple pages. Your designer can help you consider what options are best for you. In the interest of cost effectiveness, I recommend a two- or four-color brochure. The extra colors are very important because many of your customers will be visually oriented.

COPY

Your brochure copy should include four basic elements: the head, the photo captions, the subhead and the body copy. The reader will look at those elements in that approximate order.

The head, or headline, is the attention-grabber. It makes a pitch or tells what the brochure is about. If you've picked a good business name, it may be included in the head. A head makes a promise or gets attention with a clever or thought-provoking statement. It can be a question: "Are You Having Trouble Finding the Kitchen of Your Dreams?" This head might grab a homeowner who has seen too many factory cabinets in home centers. Sometimes a tagline makes a good head. For example, "Custom Cabinetry for Commercial and Residential Interiors" may not appeal to a homeowner, but its succinct, businesslike tone might attract an architectural firm.

The photo captions often are the next items read as a potential client skims your brochure, so captions are important. Captions are excellent places to drop names of satisfied customers (with permission, of course), and they can highlight services. Even a basic caption that describes the work pictured can send a message about your skills. For instance, if your brochure includes a picture of a corporate conference table, and the caption simply reads, "Custom veneered conference table for corporate headquarters, XYZ Corp.," the message to other potential corporate buyers is that you can work for the big guys. By the same standards, a homeowner who wants a library may get excited by a caption that describes library details not immediately apparent in the photo: "Mahogany library, featuring hidden multimedia cabinetry for Smith residence." Captions always get read, so I recommend using them in your brochure.

The subhead is usually found at the beginning of a section of the brochure. Readers may skim through the subheads in your brochure, seeking information that interests them. It's important that the subheads be clear and to the point. Some good examples of subheads include: Recent Work, Available Services, References, Working With a Woodworker.

The body copy fleshes out your message and includes project descriptions, project lists and your sales pitch. Tone is important. Copy that reads like a spec sheet or a comic book will turn off customers who are spending a lot of money on your services. At the same time, the brochure should be written as though you were having a conversation with the customer, explaining how you can solve problems in a professional manner. It is a good exercise to imagine you are actually writing to a specific person when you write copy.

The body copy of your brochure should also include contact information that tells the reader how to reach you. Remember to triple-check all numbers and addresses at each stage of production. Printers are not responsible for typos unless they set the type, something I do not recommend. I have seen brochures that omit phone numbers, give obscure addresses without directions or leave off contact names or work hours. The best-looking brochure in the world is useless without this vital information.

▼▼▼

WRITING THE BROCHURE

Knowing the copy elements of a brochure makes writing one less of a mystery. It's like filling in an outline. Start with the head, add the subheads, write the body copy under the relevant subhead, assemble the contact info and write captions for the photos and the illustrations. Sounds easy, doesn't it? The challenge lies in turning this dry information into a lively conversation with your readers, answering their questions, getting them excited and creating a memorable impression of you. Above all, the brochure must emphasize the benefits of hiring you and your company. It's not necessary to write huge amounts of copy for a woodworking business because your customers will be most interested the images of your work. They'll also want a checklist of the kind of projects you do and possibly some names of satisfied customers. (If you don't want to feature names in your brochure, put together a reference sheet that you can insert in your promotional package when a customer requests it.)

The brochure should answer the following questions for the reader: What problems can this woodworker solve? How will I gain from calling this person? What does it cost? Is this company reliable? Who else has used its services? These questions and more must be answered without scaring people away with clumsy or unclear writing. This is the primary reason to consider hiring a professional copywriter. A pro will greatly increase the effectiveness of your brochure.

Whether you hire a pro or decide to go it alone and write your own copy, I recommend filling out the copy questionnaire on pp. 79-83. The questionnaire will give you and/or your writer a great deal of information about your business. The completed questionnaire should save you money when working with a professional writer by reducing the amount of time the writer needs to spend learning about your business.

FINDING A WRITER

A writer who specializes in writing marketing materials like ads, brochures, sell sheets and catalogs is called a copywriter. A copywriter's job has been described as being a salesperson with a pen. A copywriter either charges by the hour or gives a set price for the job, much like the estimates you give your customers. The hourly rate ranges from $25 to $75, and the cost of a simple brochure like yours should range from $250 to $1,000. If this seems like a lot, remember that a well-written brochure will bring in work and profits, while an amateurish or poorly written piece may actually turn off customers. It is a case of using another skilled professional to maximize your investment while devoting your time to doing what you do best: woodworking.

The best way to find a writer is through a referral. If you see a brochure that works well, find out who designed the brochure by asking the business owner. A designer can often help you find a writer, and the Yellow Pages may even yield some names. Many copywriters are former ad-agency writers or new writers trying to put together a portfolio. Once you've contacted a potential writer, ask to see some work samples and find out what the writer was trying to accomplish with each piece. A copywriter should be aware of the strategy behind the piece, who it was written to and how effective the piece was. If you find someone whose work you like, consider asking some of the writer's previous clients for input. These references may save you from getting involved with someone who can't finish things. The copy will set the stage for the designer's work, so it must be the best.

Once you've chosen a writer, get a written estimate or quote that specifies exactly what will be provided and when. The estimate should include the number of versions or rewrites that may be necessary and how many meetings will be involved. A writer usually doesn't have a lot of expenses but may need things like woodworking magazines to get a feel for your business. At this point you should also pass along your completed copy questionnaire to the writer; it will be a big help in the creation of your brochure copy.

Once you have your rough copy, you will pass it to the graphic designer who will begin to assemble the brochure. He or she will help choose photos and illustrations and can get some printing quotes. I'll discuss working with designers, photographers and printers in the next two chapters.

CONSIDER TRADING YOUR SERVICES

If you simply don't have a lot of money, you may be able to trade work for work. Barter is a very effective method for woodworkers because almost everyone can think of something they'd like to have made. I've traded my copywriting skills for my maple computer desk and the shelves above it. My woodworking brother arranged to offset some of the design fees for his brochure by trading them for his design work on a kitchen remodel at the graphic designer's home. Other woodworkers I know have traded for photo shoots and printing. The best way to handle a trade situation is to have both parties estimate their work like a cash situation, then arrange the trade on that basis, making adjustments in what gets traded until both parties are happy.

One important item to consider when planning any barter or trade activity is taxation. Because some of these transactions may be subject to local, state or federal taxes, you should contact your accountant for guidance before you enter into any kind of trade agreement. Every situation is different, and you may or may not be liable in your particular situation. Your accountant or tax professional will be able to give you the type of specific professional advice that is beyond the scope of this book.

▼▼▼

THE COPY QUESTIONNAIRE HELPS FOCUS YOUR EFFORTS

When I worked as a freelance copywriter, I spent a lot of my time trying to find out exactly what my clients wanted to accomplish with their marketing plan. Often they weren't sure or didn't have the information available. So I put together a questionnaire to help my clients get organized before my expensive time started to pile up. The questionnaire was so useful that I have since used it to help many small businesses (including woodshops) organize their marketing and prepare for brochure and ad production. Make copies of the questionnaire on the next few pages and fill out a copy whenever you're working on a new brochure. Doing so will force you to think about your marketing and business from your customer's point of view. And if you're writing the brochure yourself, you'll be well on your way to understanding what your brochure or ad needs to say. Not every item on the questionnaire may be relevant to your woodworking business. But the completed questionnaire will give your copywriter and designer a good reference when they are unsure about what you want or when they need more information.

THE COPY QUESTIONNAIRE

1. Describe your business in one or two sentences.

   _____
   _____
   _____
   _____
   _____

2. What product or service is this marketing project going to promote?

   _____
   _____
   _____
   _____
   _____

3. Describe a typical customer.

   _____
   _____
   _____
   _____
   _____

4. What are the main features/skills of your business? Using the list of features, describe how each one benefits the customer. This section begins the actual copywriting process. Many of the benefits can be lifted directly off the questionnaire and used within the brochure itself.

   _____
   _____
   _____
   _____
   _____

5. What problems can you solve for your customers? These solutions don't necessarily have to have a lot to do with woodworking. The solutions you provide are based on the potential problems involved, which are often psychological things like fear of being ripped off or made to look foolish, monetary considerations and the feelings of enhanced self-esteem that

come from hiring someone to build a one-of-a-kind object. Remember you are providing a level of service that professionals pay good money for. Much of that payment is there because of your problem-solving abilities.

6. What are the goals of this marketing project?

7. Once this project is completed, what will you do with it? For example, will it be part of a direct-mail campaign? Will it be given to customers, or used to respond to requests for information? Or will it be sent out to relevant media sources to establish your expertise?

8. What are the biggest marketing problems you are facing? Contacting potential customers? Generating steady work?

9. What voice/tone/style/attitude would you like your company to project in this piece when it speaks to the customer?

10. What photos, drawings, film or audio will be used? Make an inventory of any visual items you will use for marketing.

_____

_____

_____

_____

_____

11. If photos or illustrations will be provided by you, attach brief captions describing content or action shown, location or client name, designer or job description. Keep it simple, and don't worry about wording or grammar. Include any unusual features or specifications involved. This information will help your designer sort through photos or drawings.

_____

_____

_____

_____

_____

12. List facilities, specialized tools, skills and expertise or previous experience that may be of interest to your customers; e.g., if you have an unusual tool, such as a wood-carving machine or a very large lathe, mention it. Just make sure you tell the customer why it's significant (i.e., you can make multiple copies of carved pieces or turn extra-long architectural woodwork, like porch posts or columns).

_____

_____

_____

_____

_____

13. List previous customers whose names may be used or whose names are well-known and may be used. This item is particularly important in dealing with corporations and design professionals.

_____

_____

_____

_____

_____

14. List recent projects you have done according to customer name, description of project, designer or project leader and any other pertinent information. Go back two to three years for a mix of projects that show all your capabilities. Remember your customer profile (Chapter 6)? It's a good place to start in assembling a recent projects list.

_____
_____
_____
_____
_____

15. If this marketing project focuses on a specific product or service, what other related products or services do you offer?

_____
_____
_____
_____
_____

16. What kind of guarantee do you offer for your work? How do you handle complaints or problems? And how do customers reach you when they have questions?

_____
_____
_____
_____
_____

17. List your address, phone, fax, telex, on-line number or E-mail address.

_____
_____
_____
_____
_____

18. Do you have guidelines for use of your name, logo, brands and taglines? If you do, please attach. It is important that your name and logo be used in a consistent manner to reinforce your identity in your customer's mind. You wouldn't want your name spelled differently every time someone sent you something, would you? Treat your business image the same way. Always use the same typeface, put your logo in the same relationship to your name and be consistent. These guidelines are simply rules for your designer to follow when using your name and logo. Your designer can help you define them as part of your logo-design costs.

▼ ▼ ▼

KEEPING UP WITH TECHNOLOGY KEEPS YOU IN TOUCH

If you don't have a fax machine, go out and get one. Every designer and architect out there uses faxes constantly. You'll need one for your business, and you'll save a lot of time not having to run around getting approvals on drawings.

If you have a computer and a modem, you can get an E-mail address from any on-line service.

These are rapidly replacing the use of the U.S. Postal Service (referred to as "snail mail" on-line) for mail. It also makes it possible to receive faxes on your computer, and assuming software compatibility, you could exchange electronic versions of blueprints with designers over a long distance. In the not-too-distant future, you will be sending CD-ROM versions of

your portfolio out the same way you send brochures now. (For more on CD-ROM technology, see p. 107.) These gizmos make it easy to reach potential customers anywhere on the planet. Don't deny yourself the opportunities involved because of a misguided fear of technology. These things are just tools like a hammer or router, only they're a lot less dangerous.

▼ ▼ ▼

Why use a professional photographer?

Shooting your own work

PHOTOS AND PHOTOGRAPHERS

Keeping a high-quality photographic record of your work is crucial to your business success and to the success of your marketing efforts. As a woodworker, you create beautiful, functional objects that often impact the day-to-day quality of people's lives. When a bathroom vanity is made of polished cherry and contains highly functional drawers and storage space, it improves the quality of the user's daily life. This sense of the tactile leads many people to commission custom woodworking. A professionally produced photographic record of what you do does much to convey that tactile sense to a prospective customer who is going to invest serious money into something that will be used daily. A snapshot will not do.

▼ ▼ ▼

WHY USE A PROFESSIONAL PHOTOGRAPHER?

Unless you are a competent photographer, I cannot recommend shooting your own portfolio. A professional photographer is skilled at lighting subjects to enhance detailing and patina and knows how to set up the shot to give it a dynamic presence, which makes the photo more real for the viewer. A professional photographer also knows how to balance color to adjust for artificial lighting and to make the millions of grays in a black-and-white photo appear rich and subtle. It's the same thing you do when you meticulously prepare a surface to get the look you want. Why do all that work and then use a poorly executed photo as your only record of the piece?

FINDING A PHOTOGRAPHER

How do you find and hire a photographer? Ask other woodworkers and craftspeople what photographers they use. Check with your graphic designer. He or she will have worked with many photographers and may be able to make a recommendation based on your particular needs. If all else fails, look in the Yellow Pages under "Commercial Photographers."

When you call prospective photographers, ask if they do products or people—you want a photographer who specializes in product shots. If a photographer has taken a lot of pictures of artwork, so much the better. Look at a portfolio with a critical eye. Don't be dazzled by flashy commercial shots with many darkroom effects—you don't need them, and they cost big bucks. Look for a high level of detail in shadowy areas, and make sure you see both black-and-white and color images. Also, it's important to look for well-lit detailing, clear focus all over the piece in the photo and an image that is not distorted by a cheap lens or an inexperienced photographer. A special level of quality distinguishes the extraordinary photo from the ordinary. It is difficult to define but well worth looking for. Some say a picture "pops" when it is good; others look for a kind of overall glow that is sharp and consistent. These kinds of photos show an attention to detail worthy of your work.

When you've found a photographer you can work with, try to use that person for all your shots to give a consistent look to your portfolio. Besides the studio shots, have the photographer shoot some work in progress, or keep a camera in the shop loaded with film for that time when you have an interesting jig set up or are at a complex stage of construction. To reinforce the fact that the customer is getting *your* work and skill level, make sure you or an assistant are in some shots. And make sure the photographer takes plenty of detail shots because, as architect Ludwig Mies van der Rohe said, "God is in the details."

HOW TO KEEP COSTS DOWN

Photographers usually work by the day or half day, charging from $250 to $2,500 per day. On the higher end of the scale, the price includes an assistant who can speed the process considerably. Photographers are expensive, particularly if they are good, but there are several ways to keep the price down.

Offer to barter for the services by building studio cabinetry or furnishings in exchange for the photographer's time (check with your accountant about tax liability). Another cost-cutting option is to advertise for skilled photography students and look for one who has the seeds of future ability. Student photographers need real work to include in their portfolio, and shots of artist/craftspeople's work always add pizzazz to the usual staid commercial stuff in most portfolios. The student will be cheaper. However, you get what you pay for. It may actually be more cost-effective to hire a seasoned pro who will do the work right the first time. You may have only one chance to take the photos because your future access to a piece you've made may be limited or nonexistent (e.g., the piece may have been made for a client who lives in another part of the country).

Another way to contain costs is to negotiate a lower price by offering to let the photographer shoot your piece on a day in which the photographer has nothing else scheduled. If possible, arrange to shoot several pieces during one session. This may mean rounding them up from clients or waiting until you have enough pieces to justify the cost of the shoot. Once all the pieces are in one place, it is relatively easy to shoot one after another.

PREPARING FOR THE SHOOT

You've got your photographer and have agreed to a price or rate. Now it's time for the photo shoot. There are a few things you can do to make the process efficient. Before you take the piece to the photographer's studio (which is usually cheaper than having the piece shot on site), clean and polish it until it is impeccable. Otherwise, the photographer and assistant will be doing it while the clock ticks, and you'll pay for it. Make sure every fingerprint and scuff is cleaned up—a ruined shot means starting over.

If the shoot is being done on location, remove distracting elements from the scene, leaving flowers in a simple jar or some other nondistracting object to lend scale and color to the shot. If possible, use a seamless backdrop (your photographer should have several, or you can purchase paper ones in rolls). Have the photographer take many angles and detail shots; remember, film is cheap, so don't hold back. If the piece is large, such as a big public sculpture, consider putting a person in the shot to lend scale. Keep your photos in good taste—no scantily clad models. Insist that Polaroid test photos be shot and scrutinize them with your photographer for blemishes and odd perceptual distortions. Your photographer may spot things you'd never see; a pro looks at photos all day.

SHOOTING YOUR OWN WORK

While I can't recommend shooting your own photos, there may be times when you have no other choice. Perhaps a piece is on its way out your shop door, and you must shoot it before it disappears forever. Other situations that may make it worth learning to photograph your work include catalog-type shots of any products you sell. If you design and fabricate a line of cutting boards, for instance, you'll want to photograph each item for use in catalogs, sell sheets and other marketing materials. Having a camera loaded and ready in your shop is good for those times when a great shot opportunity occurs. One of my favorite shop shots was taken just before a local woodworker was ready to send out a big architectural molding job. His shop was overflowing with assembled Victorian house parts, including railings, steps, latticework and decorative trim. It was all made of red cedar, and when we stacked it at one end of the shop, it became a great temporary display of his work. A roll of color film later, he emptied the shop, and that beautiful cedar became part of a house many miles away. The picture gets a lot of comment from people who have never seen this kind of architectural work before it's been installed on site.

YOU'LL NEED GOOD EQUIPMENT

Shooting your own stuff requires an investment of time and money on your part. Courses in photography and lighting are necessary, and you can spend a substantial amount of money for equipment. A snapshot camera won't hold up to the kind of scrutiny portfolio shots get.

You'll need a good camera, preferably a film format larger than 35mm, several high-quality lenses, a tripod and as many lighting umbrellas and fixtures as you can afford (at least three). The larger-format cameras use a big negative, which means much higher resolution when the photos are enlarged. Zoom lenses tend to distort the photo, which can make your beautiful square joinery look very peculiar. You'll need a fixed wide-angle lens of the best quality, and a longer lens for details. Skip the so-called normal lens. You'll need photo floodlights on their own collapsible stands, with folding reflective umbrellas that soften the light while allowing you to direct it, and you'll need a light meter. Add in a roll of seamless backdrop paper, and you are ready to shoot.

TAKING THE PHOTOS

Set up your piece against the seamless backdrop, arrange the lights to highlight the finish and detailing of the piece, set your exposure and take the pictures. Take a lot of photos and bracket your exposures, which means taking shots at settings both above and below those recommended by your light meter.

Try shooting from different viewpoints, open doors, pull out drawers, shoot details and place objects in the shot to lend scale. Shoot both color and black-and-white film. Use slow-speed film for better sharpness and tone with less grain. Take photos of yourself or an assistant working in your shop or on a job site.

Get the whole pile of film processed immediately and have contact sheets made so that you can select the photos you want in your portfolio (see Chapter 15). Then give the contact sheets to your designer.

If all this seems overwhelming, I admit to making it so. Unless photography is a serious hobby of yours, you'll be better off with a pro. You'll save money and get shots that will really grab the attention of your customers. Photography is not an area to be penny-wise and pound-foolish.

▼ ▼ ▼
PHOTOGRAPHY BECOMES HIGH-TECH

Desktop graphic design on computers and digital scanners that can scan a photo and make it into a computer image are important developments for small business owners. This imaging technology allows a designer to manipulate your photos, grouping different items together into one composite image, coloring or changing backgrounds, airbrushing out goofs and sharpening dark or light areas. One effective image used in a brochure I saw recently started at one side of the page as a blueprint drawing and metamorphosed into the finished piece, showing the process from idea to reality.

This technology can benefit you in several ways. Your marketing materials can have the same eye-catching images that the big guys have without stretching your limited budget. You can also salvage some poor shots of items you want featured but no longer have access to for shooting. When you contact graphic designers, ask if they can work electronically with your images. If a designer is still in the noncomputer "stone age," consider using another designer.

Chapter 12

GRAPHIC DESIGN AND PRINTING

Finding a designer

Working with a designer

Printing your materials

Once you've got your brochure copy together and have gathered a selection of visual images of your work, it is time to get together with the person who can turn these raw materials into a finished brochure: a graphic designer. Designers are skilled at assembling information into a visually compelling form that is easily understood. It often takes a designer years to develop the ability to create pieces that are effective without being gimmicky, the hallmark of excellent graphic design.

FINDING A DESIGNER

Finding a designer is just like finding a writer or a photographer. Ask for referrals from other businesses. Look at portfolios and ask why each piece is designed the way it is. Find out how effective the pieces were for the businesses that used them. Look for marketing savvy. Will the designer handle printing bids? Is the designer up to date with the latest digital design tools? How long has the designer been in business? Get several quotes and compare prices. Beware of lowball prices. A very low price is a sign that the designer either has poor business sense or is desperate. Remember, you want a marketing professional who knows how to create pieces that will sell your business effectively. If you cut corners here, you will be jeopardizing your future success as a woodworker.

WORKING WITH A DESIGNER

Here's a brief overview of what will take place once you've chosen a designer. Your designer has several tools at hand to make your message compelling. But first he or she must have a clear understanding of marketing and how the brochure fits into your plans. The designer should ask who will read the brochure and what the message is you are trying to get across. Here's where your planning will help you save money and get the best work. If your designer does not ask you about your marketing plan, find one who understands and appreciates the art of marketing.

Once the designer understands the goals of the piece, the design process can begin. Your message and images can be evaluated, and the designer will put together some rough drafts or "comps" for your approval. These comps are gradually fine-tuned until a camera-ready piece of art can be sent to a printer. Many steps take place before the printer gets the art.

The use of computers has changed the design field significantly. However, it is important to note that a computer cannot turn an untalented designer into a good one. A computer is merely a tool that facilitates the production of the work. From your point of view, a designer working with a computer is preferable because you may save money while having more options.

Nowadays, it's very unusual to find a graphic designer who is not using sophisticated page-layout programs on a daily basis. These programs take text and scanned images and allow the designer to place them in a digital layout on the screen. The programs facilitate the art of typography, which is the manipulation of type as a graphic element. By adjusting the size, separation of lines, distance of letters from each other and the font, or typeface, a designer can make your message clearer and more compelling. Most designers will use a few type styles in a piece, perhaps one for the headlines, one for the body copy and another for incidentals, like captions or quotes. The designer chooses a type for its readability and visual impact, trying to use different fonts to pull the whole piece together. The software available makes this much easier and more flexible compared to the past when the designer would spec type and have it reproduced by an outside source. Now the designer can offer you several options without costly typesetting expenses. The downside of having so many choices is the temptation to mix and match many different type styles in one piece, which is a sure sign of an inexperienced designer.

Your designer will use an electronic scanner to put your images (photos, illustrations, logo) into a computer, then maneuver the images until they fit in with the design. Numerous adjustments and special effects are available, but again, it is in your interest to be judicious with the use of these tools. You don't want a gimmicky brochure that will appear flaky or out-dated soon after it is printed.

Once the designer has a basic layout, you'll be asked to approve it and proofread for any factual errors and typos. Check and double-check at this stage. Ask someone not involved in the process to go over the copy for in-consistencies and errors (perhaps you know an English major). Make sure that names are spelled right, and that numbers are correct. Once you ap-prove the copy and the design, the designer will prepare a camera-ready file for final output.

Once the file has been assembled, your designer will take it, along with other computer files containing your scanned photos and the type soft-ware, to a service bureau. These businesses specialize in outputting high-resolution versions of your designer's work. If the piece is one color, the output will be either a glossy paper copy or a large film negative. If the piece is two or more colors, the computer software will create what is known as separations. A separation is simply a layer of film representing each layer of color. With a two-color piece, you'll see two layers of film; with four-color, you'll see four layers. The printer will then use these films or paper outputs to create the plates they use on their presses, one plate for each color. Some printers now can make plates directly from your computer files, eliminating the service bureau and thus saving you money.

While it is good to know how the process works, I usually recommend that you let your graphic designer handle all of this, coordinating each step and keeping a close eye on quality along the way. He or she has the knowledge and can communicate your interests to the pros at each step.

▼ ▼ ▼

PRINTING YOUR MATERIALS

Your graphic designer offers you another service that can save you a lot of money and aggravation: representing you when contracting with a printer to print your marketing materials. Handling this yourself is a prescription for disaster because printing is a specialized business with many arcane as-pects. Your designer should know which printers do good work and can quickly get a number of bids. Also, because the designer is a long-standing source of business for printers, he or she can twist arms when you have problems. The designer usually receives a 15% to 20% discount from the printer, which will be marked up to you as payment for the designer's ex-perience and time spent working with the printer. The deal usually still works out in your favor because the designer knows the best prices and the potential problems involved and will take the time to solve them.

Printing involves several aspects, including color, quantity, paper selection, folding, stitching (stapling), packing for shipment and the actual press run. Each is a component of the bid and are design decisions that will be made by you and your designer.

Quantity is an important issue. It is seldom cost-effective to print fewer than 1,000 copies of a piece. In fact, it usually costs almost as much to print 500 as it does to print 1,000 or more. Once a press is set up to run your print job, it is nothing to knock out another thousand or more. It is often little more than the cost of the paper. This is because you are basically paying for the setup and the labor. Once you've shelled out that initial price, it becomes very cheap to have extra copies printed. And now is the time to consider doing it, while the press is set up. If you end up needing additional brochures later, you'll have to start from scratch with the exception of the film for the printing plates, which will still exist.

Why would you want an extra thousand pieces? You might feel better about leaving them everywhere if your per-piece cost were lower, which is what happens when you go for that extra thousand or five hundred. For the few extra dollars spent, you might get enough extra brochures to bring in an extra job or two, easily justifying the cost. I believe it is worth it to splurge and print too many rather than not enough.

Once you've got the piece printed, you need to look at your plan and make sure you've considered every possible place to put those brochures. In Chapter 13, I'll show you what to do with all those boxes of paper.

YOU'VE GOT A BROCHURE, NOW WHAT?

▼ ▼ ▼

Distributing your brochures

Several boxes of your new brochure have just been delivered to your shop. The brochures look great, and you've checked them one last time for errors and printing glitches. These boxes represent a considerable investment in time and money. Now is the time to put that investment to good use, generating work and cash flow for your business. If you've stuck with me to this point, you probably already have a basic marketing plan that will help you get these marketing tools out the door and into the hands of potential customers. In this short chapter, I'm going to show you ways to use your brochures. Not every tactic will work for every shop. The idea is to start you thinking about ways to get the word out about your skills and abilities. Use the guidelines as a starting point.

I'd like to add a word of warning about those boxes of brochures. Some people I know have been unwilling to leave their expensive brochures out where any Joe Schmoe can get them. They've figured out that each one cost a certain amount of money and has a value, so they become unwilling to let the brochures go unless the reader fits certain criteria. What inevitably happens is that their brochures gather dust, and these folks complain about how the brochures didn't work. The message is: Get those brochures out of the shop and into people's hands any way you can. When your boxes start to empty, order more.

DISTRIBUTING YOUR BROCHURES

Get rid of your brochures. They are worthless in the box. If you send out a thousand and get a .5% response (5 calls), that could generate $10,000 of work—not a bad return. And you should be able to do much better than that by using your brochures to establish relationships and a referral network that generates a steady stream of business for years to come. The following is a list of possible ways to distribute your boxes of brochures.

▶ Take a pile of 50 or so, attach business cards with staples or paper clips and put them in your briefcase or a heavy envelope and keep them in your truck or car. Give a brochure to everyone you meet. You should distribute a certain number each day or week.

▶ Take a pile to every one of your local suppliers and ask if you can leave them on a counter or in the showroom. You may want to buy some wire or foamcore literature stands from a graphic-arts supply store to leave at certain locations. Other good spots to leave brochures include hardware stores, convention centers and meeting places, realty offices, home centers, lumberyards, bookstores, restaurants and libraries. Use your imagination and your knowledge of potential customers. Put yourself in their shoes and think about where you would pick up a similar brochure.

▶ Put a brochure into every piece of mail you send out, including bill payments, invoices, orders for supplies and magazine subscriptions. If a brochure doesn't fit, send a business card.

▶ Give a pile to friends and family members and offer them a finder's fee if they send a paying customer to you. Finder's fees should be at least $50 to be effective. If you have problems with this kind of incentive plan, or if it is illegal in your state, offer a dinner or gift certificate, or make something for the person.

▶ Give your lawyer, accountant, doctor, dentist, banker or piano teacher a pile and ask for referrals. I repeat: Ask For Referrals. People love to make referrals to resources they trust. The business professionals in your life exist on referrals and know that what goes around, comes around. Just make sure you always reward them and make referrals to them whenever possible. (More on referrals in Chapter 20.)

▶ Send brochures to every single media outlet in your area, including newspapers, magazines, radio and TV stations and cable operators. You'll get calls from them seeking advertising, but that is just part of the game. If they are good marketers, they'll be after you. Respect their attempts but don't give in. The best way to get media coverage is to have a name to send to and an angle for your story (more in Chapter 19).

▶ Send your brochure to competitors. Why not flaunt yourself a bit? Besides, if you enclose a note offering your specialized abilities or setups for subcontracting, you may get a steady stream of work.

▶ Come up with as many lists of potential customers as possible. Who buys woodworking? How about churches? Local store chains, restaurants, bar owners, law firms? Tool and die shops may have a need for wood components or custom casework. Many local shops need fixtures. Landmark and historical societies often make referrals for custom architectural and historical renovation work. Find out who is on the boards of these groups and send your package to every member, both at the office and at home, if possible. Use your noggin. Cruise the Yellow Pages. Keep your eyes and mind open.

▶ Send brochures to every woodworking and woodworking trade magazine along with a little description of your unique expertise. You may be able to generate interest in articles about you and your business. Also send brochures to architectural and design magazines.

▶ Offer your custom furniture-making service to local high-end furniture stores. They often have design departments. Get your brochure out to them.

▶ Three to six months after you send your initial mailing of brochures to your lists, mail them again. A second mailing is very important. Your brochure probably got glanced at but was misplaced, lost or filed. Try again and again. You are simply seeking to keep your name and business in front of potential customers until the moment they require your services. It is a memory game. You will not turn off customers with persistence. It shows that you desire success, and we all like to associate with successful people. If I'm an architect, and a woodworker sends me something interesting every month, I'll remember that woodworker when I need quotes. At the very least, I'll call for a comparison quote to check how my regular supplier is doing. And that is the foot in the door you need.

Once you've started getting one brochure out the shop door, it is time to start planning your next one. You should start taking notes about what people responded to in your latest brochure and what you'd change. A year or two from now, you'll have new work you want to highlight, new accomplishments to tell the world about, and you may have identified an entirely new niche market to focus on. At that point you'll want to target your message more specifically. The idea is to let your marketing experience refine your marketing skills the same way your hands-on woodworking experience improves your ability. You market today for tomorrow. Stop marketing today, and you won't have work in the future.

CHAPTER 14

PERSONAL CONTACT

Everything you've read up to this point has been about either planning or prospecting. You've scoped out the territory, identified prospects and begun the gradual process of making them aware of your existence and reaching out to them. The ultimate goal of most of your efforts has been to get yourself to the point where you can make personal contact with a receptive potential customer. Your brochure is paving the way through mailings and handouts. Now you have to reach out personally and introduce yourself and your business to the customer. For many, this is the scariest part of marketing.

The fear associated with marketing yourself is basic: fear of rejection. And there is only one real answer to that fear: *Don't Take It Personally.*

Negativity and rejection are seldom your fault. You have no control over what is going on in another person's mind. If you get shut down while trying to reach out to a customer, remember that it probably has nothing to do with you personally. Maybe that person had a bad day or had problems with a woodworker in the past. Maybe that person doesn't need your services right now and doesn't know how to say no politely. Maybe that person is just rotten and nasty. Whatever the story may be (and you'll probably never know), remember: *Don't Take It Personally*. I suggest you write this phrase down and post it over your desk, where you can see it when talking to problem clients or dealing with pain-in-the-neck situations.

Despite the potential pain of actually speaking to people, you must make the effort if you are going to succeed as a woodworker. You cannot lock yourself in your shop and expect people to hand you jobs over the fax machine. People don't hire woodworkers; they hire people. And the more contact you have with people, the better. There's a simple way of looking at it. When a person spends a few minutes talking on the phone with you or chatting with you at a meeting or a conference, that person starts to make a personal investment in you. He's *spent* some time. Each contact you make with that person increases his investment (and your own). When that person has a job available for a woodworker, who is he more likely to invest time and money in? You, or some guy he never met?

▼▼▼

THE PHONE

Fortunately, our society has put into universal use a tool that is ideal for making personal contact. It is nonthreatening, easy to use and easy to turn off. Everyone has one and can easily be reached with it. I am, of course, speaking of the telephone. Even the smallest woodshop can use the phone to bring in business. It may take an unprepared woodworker 200 calls, but he will eventually reach someone with a need for his services. For the woodworker who has laid the groundwork with mailings, publicity and other marketing tools, each call will have the potential to bring in profitable business.

The goal of your initial call to a prospective customer is to make an appointment to present the facts about your business. Usually this means getting together to show your portfolio or to discuss a job. (Chapters 15 and 16 will help you prepare for that presentation.) You aren't calling to chat. You're not trying to make a presentation over the phone or on the spot. Your goal is to get out your calendar book and make an appointment to meet. This step is vital to your success as a prospector seeking work.

As part of your marketing plan, you'll be doing mailings and following up with telephone calls on a regular basis, perhaps three to five per day. Pick a specific number of completed calls as a goal and don't stop until you've reached that goal. Make calls every day. Early in the morning is a good time. Your goal should be to make at least one appointment per week to present your business to a prospective customer. If you can stick to this, you'll meet and develop a relationship with at least 50 possible sources of business per year. That should be enough to generate plenty of business, particularly when a customer means repeat business and/or referrals.

If it takes 15 calls to get an appointment, and three appointments to get a job worth $1,000, then each call is worth $22 (15x3=45. $1,000÷45=$22). Thinking of it this way may make you a little more motivated to make those calls! Three calls per day should not take more than an hour, and $66 bucks an hour is not bad money.

WHO DO YOU CALL?

Like your mailings, you'll be working from a list or lists. Your primary list is your past and present customers. They should be called regularly. Make sure they've gotten your mailings and ask them what they think of the mailings. Enlist these people as allies who are valued sources of input into your business. By getting them involved in your marketing, as informal consultants, you will flatter them and generate referrals. You may even get some good marketing advice or leads toward other potential customers.

The second list will be targeted customers whose profile most closely fits your ideal customer. This call is harder than calling a previous customer because you have not yet established personal contact or developed a relationship. You are just one more person trying to sell them something. Everything you do to promote yourself prior to the call will increase the likelihood of success with these "cold" calls. If they've seen your brochure, heard of your work or read about you, they'll be far more likely to take your call. Even if they haven't heard of you, your target marketing should match their interests and yours.

GETTING PAST GATEKEEPERS

Gatekeepers are the secretaries and the assistants whose jobs include screening calls. When you talk to these very important persons, remember that if anyone has read your brochure, it is probably the gatekeeper. Be friendly, make note of the person's name and be sure to use it every time you call. You should smile when you speak on the phone. Your mood is conveyed over the phone by your tone, pacing and breathing. You should be relaxed and professional. Remember, these people are mere humans like yourself, doing their jobs. If you can't get through, leave a message. Say something like, *"This is Chris Zyslinski from Arcadia Woodworks. Would Mr. Smith please return my call?"* Try again the next day.

If the gatekeeper doesn't know who you are, ask if the information you sent out has arrived. If the answer is no, ask the gatekeeper personally if you can send the information again, marked to his or her attention. And do it right away. One way around gatekeepers is to call very early or after five o'clock, when these hourly employees are not there. Often you'll get your prospect on the phone right away.

WHAT DO YOU SAY?

There is a proven method that helps you get through your initial nervousness and achieve your objective of getting an appointment. Use a script. It will help immensely when you get nervous or suddenly forget what you want to say. It doesn't mean you have to say it word for word; it simply gives you a reference point and a checklist to follow to make sure you stay aimed at your goal and don't forget anything important, like your phone number or who you are talking to.

A typical script for making an appointment might read like this.

> *Hello, this is Max Gert calling for Mr. Armor.*
>
> *Yes, Mr. Armor, my name is Max Gert, and I'm a partner at Arcadia Woodworks. We sent you some information about our woodworking business recently, and I wonder if you've had a chance to take a look at it.*
>
> *We're a full-service custom woodshop, and I'm calling to see if we can get together so that I can show some of the things we've done for other designers. It'll take only about 10 minutes of your time. Are you free on Tuesday afternoon next week? How about Friday at two? A week from Monday? Great. I'll see you then. My number is 000-0000 in case you need to reschedule. Thanks, and have a good day.*

Whether your brochure has been received or read is irrelevant once you have a prospective customer on the phone. Your goal is to get an appointment. Don't give a sales pitch or offer to send more materials. Don't get bogged down to a long-winded description of your business. If the person asks you to send materials, say fine and then go for the appointment. Always have a specific day and time in mind, and if those are no good, find an alternative. You must assume that the meeting will be set up. Leave your number only as a courtesy in case the person has to reschedule. Never use the word cancel.

If the customer is not interested, politely say thank you and go on to your next call. Don't spend any additional energy on definite no answers. Always stay polite, even if someone is rude or unpleasant. Remember, *Don't Take It Personally*. And you'll be amazed at how keeping your cool and sticking to your guns chills out even the hottest customer.

NETWORKING

Networking conjures up images of people in business suits exchanging business cards while making deals left and right. In fact, your local chamber of commerce probably organizes networking get-togethers that resemble this image. Unfortunately, if you've ever attended these kinds of functions, you've probably found yourself standing around trying to look businesslike while your crisp pile of cards sits in your pocket. That's because networking doesn't work as an activity in itself. It comes about because of a shared interest among people who meet while pursuing that interest. Perhaps the best metaphor I can generate is that of a small town.

If you live in a small town, you know that everyone has a way of knowing everyone else and their business. If Joe Jones needs a plumber, his wife gets a name from her hairdresser. If Sally Marks wants to go into business as a graphic designer, she spreads the word within the town, enlisting her friends and relatives to get started. The network is functioning.

Within every community, no matter how large and diverse, there are many small towns that share a common interest instead of a geographical location. Artists tend to know everyone in the art scene. Builders keep track of each other's business as a matter of course through gossip, trade news and the network. Your goal is to find the community that represents the interests of your best customers and join that community. Once you are in and active, your name will be spread around by word of mouth. And word of mouth is what networking is all about.

GO WHERE THE CUSTOMERS ARE

The number-one rule of networking is to identify where your customers are likely to congregate and go there. If you are a fine-arts woodworker, you must attend as many functions as possible, including gallery openings, fund-raisers, invitational and open shows, master classes and art auctions. Your goal is to get to know the movers and shakers in the art scene. Eventually, you'll get to know the subgroup of people who buy and sell fine craftwork, and they will get to know you. At that point, you will be going after the ultimate goal of your networking: making an appointment to familiarize the other person with you and your work. Sounds familiar, doesn't it? And you didn't even have to put on a suit.

Where do you go to network? Take classes taught by architects. Go to builder's association meetings as a guest (just call and ask if you can attend). Join your landmark or historical society and attend all the meetings. Get involved in the building committee of your church. Put together a brief presentation on working with a custom woodworker and offer to speak at meetings for free. Make sure you use a lot of slides and keep your talk benefit oriented. Check the business section of your paper for upcoming business gatherings that might be places to meet customers. Make sure that they might have a role in buying decisions. You wouldn't want to attend a meeting of information systems managers unless you are a builder of computer furniture, but you might want to try a facilities-planning conference. Teaching classes at your local night-school program, or even at a university or college, is a good way to meet possible customers. Just make sure you teach courses attended by adults because of their interest in the field. If your main customers are individuals rather than commercial buyers, almost any classroom situation can put you in touch with potential business. A class in Japanese gardening at a local museum might lead to a job building a teahouse or a kitchen.

No matter where you go to meet people, you must have a plan. Bring cards and brochures. Take an interest in the subject of the gathering. Always get yourself seated at tables full of people you don't know. And never attend with a partner, unless you plan ahead to split up. You'll end up huddling together as a unit, and a single person is much more approachable than two. Avoid people you know, unless they are active or potential customers. If you see someone you know and would like to develop a business relationship with, say hello, chat a minute and then make a lunch date. Go on to the others around you.

The key to meeting and starting relationships with others is to take an interest in what they do. Ask your tablemates or neighbors what they do. Ask them about the challenges and the responsibilities they face. If they ask you what you do, have a one-sentence description ready, say it and let them ask questions. Listen for opportunities. Remember that you are not a woodworker; you are a problem-solver. Once you've established an easy relationship, you might ask people if they've ever used a custom woodworker. Don't push it. When the conversation is winding down, or you get interrupted, tell them you enjoyed meeting them, offer your card and get theirs. If circumstances warrant it, suggest getting together to talk about each other's business or needs. At this point you have made a personal contact, started an investment of time on their part and gotten informal permission to contact them (they gave you a card with their contact info on it). If you can, leave them a brochure. I've found that almost everyone has an interest in seeing pictures of skilled craftsmanship.

Follow-up after a networking opportunity is essential. You aren't going after just one opportunity; you are trying to establish a presence in a community. Even if you gave a brochure to someone, send another piece the next day, with a note saying you enjoyed meeting and talking with that person. Put these prospects on your list and call to set up an appointment to show your work. Remember that even if a person does not have a need for woodworking right now, he or she probably knows someone else who does. By maintaining and building a personal investment in you, your networking contacts will take an interest in your prosperity.

But networking is a two-way street. Everyone is doing his own form of networking. By reaching out to others, you give them opportunities to benefit from your relationship. You'll meet potential resources. You may be able to refer others to them for business. Once you've become a potential source of business, you are much more likely to get referrals. Don't hesitate to ask for them.

Establishing personal contact and building business relationships are the keys to success in any small business. It is doubly important in a business that offers customized skills like woodworking. You are selling service and problem-solving ability. People must feel they can rely on you. Personal connections are the best way to convey that sense of reliability. Remember that you never sell your services to organizations or companies; you are always selling to a *person*. Even if the checks come from a Fortune 500 company, an individual made the decision to sign them. You must seek out and meet people and get to know them one on one. That is the value of picking up the phone or joining a club and attending meetings.

YOUR PORTFOLIO

Your portfolio is your record of accomplishments as a woodworker. It acts as a portable showroom and demonstrates to a potential customer that you can take a project from initial concept to finished product. It is an expanded resume, showing who you have worked for and with, and what kinds of abilities you have. If carefully maintained, your portfolio can be an effective marketing tool, flexible enough to work in a variety of selling situations. Poorly done, however, it can hurt your business by giving the impression of shoddiness or lack of attention to details. Because your portfolio is so important, I am going to spend this chapter on the mechanics of assembling and using a portfolio as a marketing tool.

▼ ▼ ▼

ASSEMBLING A PORTFOLIO

Many woodworkers take a gimmicky approach to their portfolio. They haul around miniature cabinetry, models and elaborate toolboxes in the manner of the 19th-century craftsman, whose toolbox was a demonstration of his abilities. Well, all of these crafty approaches will get attention, but they detract from the ultimate use of a portfolio as a marketing tool. We live in times when we have access to all kinds of technologies that allow us to store a visual record of our work. To put it bluntly, a portfolio should consist of carefully chosen photographs of your work in a format that is professional, from a business point of view, and portable. Ditch the gimmicks and let the photos tell the story.

In Chapter 11 I showed you how to get your work on film and, ultimately, into your portfolio. I'll reemphasize a few points: Shoot everything you do before you lose touch with it. Put something in the shots to lend scale and perspective. Take process shots while you work, using them to highlight any special abilities or tools you have. Whenever possible, include shots of your work in its final context, i.e., completed kitchens, furnishings in the rooms they were designed for and commercial work being used at the place of business.

Once your photos are shot, have 8x10 glossy prints made and put them in a binder, or you can dry-mount them on slightly larger mounting boards. While you are doing this, have at least three copies of each shot prepared for your portfolio and have additional prints made, if possible, for those times when a customer requests a copy. Always give a nicely finished copy of the picture to the owners of the piece and get their permission, in writing, to use the image and their names in your promotional materials. Buy three decent-quality zipper portfolio binders and assemble three portfolios because you may have to leave a portfolio with a client or mail one to a customer who's out of your area.

Besides photos, you may include other elements in your portfolio, such as copies of your brochure or postcards, pictures of your shop, copies of your construction drawings or renderings and copies of articles about or by you. Once you've assembled all these things, your portfolio will start to be the effective marketing tool it should be. Then you can get to the fine-tuning stage.

▼▼▼

CUSTOMIZING YOUR PORTFOLIO

I am always surprised by how poorly organized many portfolios are. Too often, a portfolio is a mishmash of projects and miscellaneous information thrown together without rhyme or reason. For your portfolio to be an effective presentation tool, you must organize it differently for each presentation you are making.

Most businesses that involve selling services or products have some kind of sales presentation. It can range from a simple demonstration to an elaborate audio-visual extravaganza, featuring orchestral music and live action video. These presentations are important because they reach out to all of the customer's senses, including sight, sound and feelings, both emotional and physical. Your portfolio also should be an adaptable presentation, with elements appealing to all the senses. Your photos convey visual information, and they often appeal to your customers by showing glowing surfaces and a range of textures that cry out to be touched and used. The way you present your portfolio will add an aural dimension, which you control by your choice of words, tone, volume and pacing.

Consider the job you are going after and arrange your portfolio accordingly. If it is a commercial cabinetry job, for example, emphasize the cabinetry work you've done for other businesses and include only one or two residential jobs (your business customer may want a library installed at home!). Make sure the portfolio shows relevant skills like installation ability or specialized shop tools, such as a veneer press or a spray booth. Keep the portfolio brief and to the point. You will find that most customers don't really want to know about everything you've done; they want to know if you can do the job *they* want.

SHOWING YOUR PORTFOLIO

A potential customer who looks at your work may skip pieces that are your favorites and may instead be turned on by things you considered leaving out. Don't grouse about the customer's lack of taste; simply consider the meeting as an information-gathering session. Ask why the customer is interested in this picture or that and listen for clues to what he or she needs. Once you identify the needs and wants of the client, tailor your presentation to those wants, skipping less relevant topics. For instance, if you notice a lot of interest in the granite shelves that were a part of a corporate wall unit, emphasize your ability to act as a resource for a wide variety of materials, rather than trying to steer the customer's attention back to the fine veneering you did on the same project. He or she may have been thinking of using an exotic material but had held back because of fears that it might slow down the project or become a big hassle. Your ability to turn those fears into something easily handled might win you the job.

When you show your portfolio, you are showing how you used creative problem-solving to create beautiful things. When you show a kitchen, don't talk about the complex joints in the drawers or the trouble you had with the installation; talk about how the new design changed the owners' lives, making them rediscover the joy of cooking and eating at home. Remember to stress benefits over features. You may look at a photo and remember that it took three months to get paid for a set of chairs, but your customer sees a potential improvement to his or her lifestyle.

Many woodworkers tend to leave out work that is old or work they no longer are interested in. But remember, some potential clients have not seen your work, and an old piece may appear fresh and relevant to their needs. If you are being asked to bid on a table, load your portfolio up with all the tables you've done. If you haven't done many tables, include other freestanding furnishings or pieces that use the same skills as making a table would.

When you meet your customer for the first time and make your presentation, follow the sales tactics in Chapter 16. Ask questions and listen, interrupting only to ask more questions and to keep the conversation on the important subject: your customer. Show an interest in the customer's business and find out what the customer looks for in a craftsperson. Only after you have a rapport with the customer and sense what he or she is like should you show the portfolio. Say that you'd like to show a few things you've done that might be interesting. Don't launch into a sales pitch. Just take out each shot and give a brief history of the project: what it is, who you did it for, how they used or liked it. If you can't use specific, recognizable names, use a demographic description: "This is a mahogany cabinet containing an entertainment system that I built for the home of a local executive. It has a 27-in. TV on a powered elevator, a VCR and a stereo that all work from one universal remote. When not in use, they disappear into the cabinet, and all you see is a piece of fine furniture."

Stop and let the client react. Then go on to the next picture. Keep the show short and limit your presentation to eight to 10 pieces or less. Once you are finished with the presentation, ask the customer to keep you in mind for future quotes and say you can be called anytime with questions or for a fast quote. Make sure you leave your phone and fax numbers. If you don't have a fax, arrange to use someone else's and start saving for your own. (It's fairly easy and inexpensive to add a fax to a desktop computer, if you already own a computer.) Almost half the jobs my brother bids on these days come over the fax machine.

Your portfolio and its use as a presentation tool will become very important as your sales skills develop. In the next chapter, I'll be looking at that most feared of all creatures, the salesperson, and how you can turn yourself into an effective member of the club without selling your soul or wearing polyester suits.

▼ ▼ ▼
TECHNOLOGY
AND YOUR
PORTFOLIO

Breakthroughs in imaging technology are changing the way many artists and artisans are using their portfolios to market themselves. Eastman Kodak's Photo CD technology makes it possible for you to put your entire portfolio on a CD-ROM disk, which is similar to a compact disk. Most large photo labs can take your slides and pictures and put them on a Photo CD for $20 to $40. Many images can be held on one CD, and with the help of a Photo CD player or a CD-ROM player, the images can be shown on a television or a computer screen. You can arrange your images any way you like, and the images can be easily cropped or turned. Graphic designers can take these images off your disk and use them with desktop publishing software.

This high-tech stuff is important because it makes it easy to duplicate your portfolio, send it out to distant customers and to provide photos to magazines, graphic designers or anyone else in a position to promote your work. As Photo CD players become more common (most designers and architects have them now) and duplication costs go down, you'll be able to send your portfolio out the same way you mail a brochure now. Your customers may put together databases of vendors that require you to use similar technology. In any case, Photo CD is an excellent way to store your images for the near future when this technology will be commonplace.

▼ ▼ ▼

Selling is problem-solving

Basic sales training

DEVELOPING SALES SKILLS

Fear of selling is probably the number-one problem facing small-business owners. Many people distrust salespeople and assume that those who sell make their living cheating people and gloating over it. Yet, if you look at the chief executives of large companies, you'll find that many of them have sales backgrounds. Big business values sales ability. Without effective salespeople, any large company would be out of business.

As the owner of a small business, you must develop sales skills, too. You will eventually learn through experience, but this is slow and expensive. I've watched woodworkers lose customers and bids because of their inability to recognize signals a customer is sending. Sales training helps you recognize when the customer is asking for something you aren't providing. I'm going to cover some sales basics in this chapter, but I highly recommend reading the books in the Resource section on p. 150 and taking one or more sales-training seminars whenever you can. You'll find out about these seminars in your local newspaper business sections and in the catalogs of local colleges. Also, local business associations like the chamber of commerce sponsor events (i.e., sales-training seminars). The things you learn will be put to use daily as you deal with new clients, as you work with current customers and as you prospect for more work.

SELLING IS PROBLEM-SOLVING

Identify the problems your potential customer is facing, find a solution to them, and you will get the job. Sounds simple, right? In fact, it is a fairly simple concept, but we often get confused during the sales process and lose track of the customer's concerns. That is why professional salespeople have developed a process they go through every time they sell. Knowing the steps involved allows a salesperson who starts to lose control of the sale get back on track. The four steps a professional follows are:

► Prospecting and meeting the potential customer.

► Learning about the customer and the customer's needs.

► Addressing those needs in a presentation.

► Completing the sale and following up.

BASIC SALES TRAINING

This whole book is about finding potential sources of business. I've expanded the points above and developed a program called Basic Sales Training. This six-step program teaches people who are not full-time salespeople enough about selling to get the job done. I recommend that you and all your employees become familiar with sales techniques. The program will give your small business an edge on the competition, particularly in a craft like woodworking, where few practitioners have any formal sales training. Basic Sales Training is simple and will introduce you to the art and craft of selling—anyone can learn it.

This training program assumes you already have a "lead," or introduction, to a potential customer through one of the various marketing techniques I introduced in this book. You sent out a brochure or left a business card, and one day the phone rings; it is someone interested in having some work done. What do you do?

STEP 1: MEET AND GREET

Meet and Greet is a term used in the car business. It conjures up images of some guy in a polyester suit sticking out a beefy hand for a shake while sizing up your financial situation at a glance. Stereotypes like this have caused a lot of effective salespeople to take a long look at how to make a good first impression. Meet and Greet is often a brief step, but it does set the stage for your future dealings with the customer. In your case, as a woodworker, this contact may happen twice with each potential customer—once on the phone and once in person. You can ensure that you will make a good impression by taking a few precautions.

The phone

How do you answer the phone? Do you say, "Yeah?" How about "Hello?" Or how about "Woodshop!" I've heard all of these and many more equally terrible answers. These people are telling me, the potential customer, that I am pretty unimportant; in fact, I'm not even worth identifying themselves or their business to. These answers get me thinking. Maybe you're not identifying your business because of collection agencies on your tail. Or maybe I got the wrong place. Maybe this guy on the other end is going to be an ignorant lout and nothing but trouble. I don't want that. In fact, because I'm going to be spending a lot of money and time on this project, maybe I better call somebody who's more professional and dependable.

This is no exaggeration. Remember, selling is problem-solving and you don't want to sound like a potential problem on the first encounter. The solution is easy. Have a standard way of answering the phone and always use it. Two examples: "Arcadia Woodworks, Max speaking," or "Hello, Arcadia Woodworks. How can I help you?" Make sure everyone uses the same response. Then make sure you don't lose the call, which is easy if it's just you in the shop. If you don't work alone, make sure everyone in the shop knows that all incoming calls are important, and don't put people on hold for more than a few seconds. Take accurate messages and always return calls as soon as you can. Fast responses to calls let customers know they are important.

So, you're on the phone with Fred Smith, a new customer, and he is impressed by your professional demeanor. He tells you something about his project and asks you a few questions about your experience. You offer to send out a brochure and then make an appointment to meet. Finally, he asks if you've ever worked with an obscure colored plywood from Finland that the architect wants to use. Stop right here.

If you have never heard of the stuff, don't tell him otherwise. Say you're not familiar with it, but you'll try to get some information about it before the meeting. He says great, and you hang up.

There are a few important lessons here. One, you made an appointment. Always go for the personal meeting, unless the customer lives far away. In that case, send or fax the information, then call to see if there are any questions. The second lesson is the, "I don't know" answer. Don't be afraid to admit that you don't know the answer to a question, but be sure to tell the customer that you'll get more information about the subject. A simple, honest response is, "I don't know, but I'll find out and get back to you."

This brings up the price question. Some people will want estimates on the phone. Don't do it. When customers ask for price ranges, tell them you will look over the project and get back to them. If they insist on a price, tell them estimates take time, and it would not be fair to give a figure that was too low or too high. (For more on quotes and estimates, see Chapter 18.) Remember these magic words: "I'll get back to you."

The meeting

You've conveyed a good sense of professionalism on the phone and have set up a meeting. You're now in the next "first-impression" stage. You'll be meeting Fred and his architect, Sheila Jones, at Sheila's studio. You work all morning in the shop, sanding, and then rush to the meeting. You're a little dusty, you've got a crummy pair of pants on, and you're a little disorganized, but hey, you made it, didn't you? You walk in, and the architect is sitting in her suit, her client is here between his meetings at the office, and you look like something the cat dragged in. But it's okay because you're the crafty type, and a little sawdust just says you're for real, right? Wrong.

If someone drops into your shop, and you're a mess, fine. If you're meeting a customer anywhere, and you have advance notice, clean up your act. This may not mean a suit, but it does mean clean clothes, decent shoes and a clean shop if that's the meeting place. First impressions, remember? If you come across as organized and relatively prosperous, you won't telegraph a negative message to the client.

In this example you have a double whammy because you are meeting two potential sources of future business: the architect and her client. Your custom woodworking skills are expensive, so in general, you'll be dealing, with businesses and individuals that are successful. These affluent people are worth far more to you than a single, small job. They represent a continuous stream of referrals and future business if you treat them right. It is also very likely they have been burned by a contractor in the past or know someone who has. Your professionalism and that good first impression help allay any of the customer's fears of giving money to a stranger and receiving shoddy merchandise, or worse, in return.

STEP 2: QUALIFYING

The next step in Basic Sales Training is Qualifying, which is the process of gathering information about the needs and wants of your customer. If this step is done well, the rest will easily fall into place.

The secret to Qualifying is to listen and take notes, mental or otherwise. Listen for clues from the customer that point to past experiences, financial limitations, style and color preferences, usage and personal dislikes. You must resist the temptation to show your wares and expertise. Only ask enough questions to get the customer talking and guide the conversation back to the project at hand when it veers away. At this stage you are gathering information about the nature of the problem or problems that face the customer. Each problem represents an opportunity because, if you can provide a solution, you come that much closer to the sale. Let's go back to the example.

Sheila begins by telling you about the project. In this case, it's a built-in audio-visual cabinet in a new residence. She has drawings and everything is spec'd out, including that colored Finnish plywood. Another part of the job calls for a purple dye over mahogany veneer, which, she explains, matches some existing furnishings. During the conversation you make some notes, ask questions and show some samples of the plywood you had delivered from a distributor in New Jersey.

This is where (and this is a situation based on an actual event) the know-it-all woodworker jumps in and says, "That purple dye is not going to work. Are you sure that's what you want?" A much better approach is to restrain yourself and just listen. Unless you are being paid for your design expertise, don't second-guess the architect. It's her job, and while she may or may not know what she is doing, now is not the time to be negative. If you think that most architects can't possibly know as much as you, the craftsperson, then perhaps you should consider building only your own designs. It is not a joke when people say the customer is always right.

Back to the meeting. Fred says that he must have this done by a certain date because he is having a party for his business partners. He also says his wife, Susan, must approve the finishes and wants to know if you do installations. Can you do the wiring and the lighting within the unit?

Before you start responding, let's look at what this qualifying situation has told you. You now know the following:

► There is a deadline.

► The client's wife is a decision-maker. Direct your answers to her concerns, too.

► Many potential customers will see your work if you get the job.

► The finish is not negotiable, and matching that existing furniture is a key to getting the job. Ask for a sample or to see the pieces you must match to head off potential problems. By setting up a meeting at Fred and Susan's house, you accomplish two things: You meet the wife, and the clients have invested more time with you personally. This will predispose them to your bid (if they like you!).

► The ability to do the installation and the wiring will move you up the list. I call these extra skills profit centers (more about profit centers in Chapter 21).

Keep your ears open for clues about what will get you the job. By identifying and addressing the problems you and the customer face, you'll be able to command a higher price and still get the job. Attend meetings with a notepad in hand and make a list of potential problems and concerns involved in the project. This list will ensure that you cover all the bases and will mark you as a professional. Once you've learned as much as possible about the project, you can go on to the next step: Presentation.

STEP 3: PRESENTATION

Present your expertise to the customer using a feature/benefit approach. Rather than just opening your portfolio and rambling on about what you've done in the past, you should tailor your presentation to the customer's situation. This is relatively easy if you have done a good job qualifying and listening.

Feature/benefit selling is a very important concept. Understanding the difference between features and benefits can make the sale. Many small businesses place too much emphasis on features and not enough on benefits. Take a good look at your list of marketable products (see Chapter 7) and consider which will benefit this customer most. This list becomes a very important marketing tool. In your sales presentation and marketing materials, you will always emphasize the benefit over the feature. Whenever you mention a feature, you must immediately describe the correlating benefit. Back to the example:

You might start by showing Fred and Susan photos of AV cabinetry you have done and explain what you learned that applies to their job. Get out the plywood samples and explain that you have found a supplier that will save money on this very expensive material. Also explain that using the plywood will actually save more money because it eliminates some of the finish expense. (This makes the architect who specified it look good, which is good for future business.) Explain how you specialize in matching existing finishes; in fact, this is mentioned in your brochure, along with a description of your expertise as an installer. Give everyone at the meeting a brochure now, even if they have one. Ask Sheila some informed questions about the wiring and the lighting, displaying your knowledge by relating the questions to the particular problems posed by the project being discussed. Mention that you have resources for certain built-in hardware and that you'll fax the specs to her when you get back to the shop. Set up the appointment to see the site for measurements. There are a couple of details you need more information about, and you agree to check them out and get back to Sheila. End of meeting.

Your presentation was not a listing of your accomplishments or bragging about your expertise. Instead, it addressed the immediate concerns, or problems, of the customers, methodically eliminating or handling those concerns. Try to solve problems during the presentation stage. As you gain more sales experience, you will become more comfortable at presentations. If you are inexperienced, practice with a friend who plays the devil's advocate. If you can get into a good sales-training course, you and others will act out various aspects of the sales process. Role-playing is very valuable for any businessperson.

STEP 4: TRIAL CLOSE

In sales, the "close" is the point at which you ask for the job. Amazingly, a lot of businesspeople fail to close the deal because they never ask for the job! They just can't bring themselves to ask. Ironically, experience shows that people want to be guided by the salesperson and need that direct question to make their decision. The Trial Close is a dry run done before you make the final request for a job. There are several reasons for having a trial close.

First of all, the Trial Close helps you identify any problems that still need to be solved or addressed. Allow the customer to make a conditional answer. For instance, you might say: "If we can iron out the problem with the electrician, when would you like me to get started?" This statement is basically saying that, aside from this problem, would you be willing to hire me? This will bring any other issues out into the open.

The customer might respond by saying: "Yes, if we can agree on a price and if you can guarantee you'll be finished before our party on the fifth."

The Trial Close allows you to take the temperature of the situation. You'll find out if the person you've been presenting to is actually the decision-maker, you'll find out about potential competition, and you'll find out what the real priorities are. This step is really another part of the information-gathering process.

If you address all of the customer's problems during both the Presentation and the Trial Close, you'll more than likely get a verbal commitment from the customer.

STEP 5: THE CLOSE

The Close is basically a process of tying up loose ends and getting a written commitment from the customer (a contract) and a down payment. If this is a bidding situation, all of your sales efforts were aimed at cementing your relationship with the person soliciting the bid and using your expertise to steer the bid away from a strictly low-ball price situation. An effective sales presentation will build value and more profit into your work. (More about the whole bidding process in Chapter 18.)

Closing is often portrayed as the final step in the sales process. This is a fundamental mistake. The final step, Follow-Up, will really ensure that everything goes well.

STEP 6: FOLLOW-UP

After you close on the sale, the work begins, but you have another step to take. You must follow up with the customer. Call and thank Fred and Susan (and Sheila) for the business and update them on their project. Saying thank you in some way really leaves a good impression. However, good follow-up has an even more important function.

Word of mouth is the mainstay of all small-business marketing. An essential component of word of mouth is referrals and recommendations. Follow-up after the job is completed will lead to referrals if the customer is satisfied. Follow-up during the job will ensure satisfaction. You should be methodical about follow-up. If you say you'll get back to the customer with some information, do it right away. If he wants a bid on something else, have it on his desk the next day. People are used to not having promises kept, so you will look like a real problem-solver if you develop a reputation for getting things done now rather than later. And remember, selling is problem-solving.

As a last note to the Basic Sales Training, I'd like to mention referrals again. Ask for referrals and ask again every three months. Just call up and say you're calling to say hello, checking to see if everything is holding up and asking to keep you in mind if the customer hears about anyone who needs work done. It's as simple as that, but it will generate a lot of business.

ADVERTISING

You may have noticed that I have not talked about advertising much in this book. This omission may surprise a lot of people who think advertising and marketing are the same. Of course, by now you probably understand that advertising is only one facet of marketing. I have not put a great deal of emphasis on advertising because it can be very expensive and must be used over a long period of time to be really effective. However, there are times when advertising may be an important marketing tool.

▼ ▼ ▼

SHOULD YOU ADVERTISE?

There are several situations where advertising will be effective for your woodworking business. To understand why these situations justify the expense of an ad campaign, it is important to understand the basics of advertising. First of all, the advertising I'll be talking about in this chapter will be print advertising. You may eventually want to run radio or TV spots, especially with the proliferation of cable channels. However, the effective use of the broadcast media requires a sophisticated understanding of media buying and commercial production, and that is beyond the scope of this book. Such advertising also tends to be very expensive.

Print ads reach a very large, general-interest audience. If placed in trade publications or other specialized publications, they can raise your profile and may bring in new business. If you specialize in large commercial projects or offer a consumer-oriented service like kitchen and bath design and fabrication, you will probably find ads effective. However, you must be able to handle enough work to justify the expense of the ads and to satisfy the customers they pull in. A deluge of work that your shop cannot handle means you've not only wasted money, but you've also soured many potential customers on your business.

An effective ad must be part of a campaign, appearing frequently and consistently. If Chris and Max wanted to try advertising Arcadia Woodworks in a local business magazine, I'd ask them the following questions:

▶ Will you commit to running at least 12 consecutive ads?

▶ Can you afford it? In Arcadia's case, a small black-and-white display ad would cost about $175 per month. That expense would probably become part of Arcadia's monthly overhead.

▶ Can you handle a large influx of bids and work that could result from the ads? The magazine Arcadia was considering is aimed at the local business community. The goal would be to build awareness of the business and get larger commercial jobs. Chris and Max could probably handle the amount of work by carefully planning and possibly outsourcing work.

▶ Will you keep the same message and format for all of your ads to maintain a consistent image and identity?

Ads must deliver a consistent message. The graphic designer Chris and Max used for their brochure had already done a few rough versions of ads using the style and copy that was used in Arcadia's brochure. While there are three different images used in the ads, they all use the same format and similar copy.

All of these points are vital. Readers must see an ad repeatedly before they are likely to act upon it. The first few times the ad may only be noted in passing. After the ad appears regularly in the magazine, the reader feels a sense of recognition. Eventually the ad will become a memorable message for a company that has staying power. The company will become a potential resource for customers who are considering a sizable expenditure on a woodworking project. Unfortunately, most business owners either give up on their advertising too early or constantly fiddle with it, changing messages and appearance in a futile attempt to make it "work." This is like starting over again every couple of months, throwing your previous ad budget down the drain. If you advertise, be frequent and consistent.

▼▼▼

CREATING EFFECTIVE ADVERTISING

The lessons you learned while producing your brochure are valuable when you put together an ad. Often, the headline you used in the brochure, a good photo, a caption, a list of specialties and your logo and contact information are enough to create an effective ad. You really need a good graphic designer who can make an ad stand out. He or she will work within the publication's technical specifications to make sure your ad looks its best.

In general, you won't generate enough ad billings to keep an ad agency interested in your account. However, your graphic designer may act as a small agency, receiving a discount, typically 15%, in exchange for bringing in your business. A designer earns this discount by dealing with the publication(s) and ensuring that the ads appear without errors.

A less expensive option is to place a classified ad in a publication. Most publications charge by the number of words (a headline will add to the cost), and your ad will be placed in the classified section of the publication under a heading. For example, a woodshop's ad might appear under the heading, "Custom Woodworking." This could be a very cost-effective method of telling potential customers about the services you offer.

PICKING YOUR MEDIA

Where your ads appear is the most important decision of an advertising campaign. Media are judged by the size of their audiences. When you express interest in buying advertising space, a salesperson will show you all kinds of statistics on the publication(s). The important thing to remember here is that you still want to target your optimum customer. If you build AV cabinetry, you will advertise in magazines or trade publications read by designers and buyers of AV cabinetry. An ad in your local newspaper would not only be ineffective, but it would also be very costly.

If you read *The New Yorker,* you've probably seen ads for Thos. Moser, Cabinetmaker. These ads are very effective and built his small business into a large furniture factory. Now we are seeing many imitators in the pages of that magazine and other similar publications. While imitation is a tried-and-true advertising tactic, I doubt these imitators have the means to profit from these very expensive ads. Moser had to build factories to generate the volume of business that makes his ads worthwhile. This kind of mass-market advertising is not for a small woodshop. I recommend sticking to niche publications that are read by your specialized audience. The rates are often lower, and the readers will be more likely to respond to your ads.

Consider the many national trade magazines that cater to specialized markets like architects, designers, space planners, sculptors and artists, office design, kitchen and bath design. The number of specialized publications is mind-boggling. A visit to your local library's information desk will put you in contact with many publication directories. If the library has the Standard Rate and Data directories, you can even get an idea of the cost of the various ads. These directories may help you find a profitable niche area. If a magazine interests you, call and ask for a sample copy and media kit. If someone asks if you have an agency, give your designer's name. You might get a discount out of it. Read the magazines and look through back issues for ads by businesses similar to your own. Go back several issues and check to see if the ads have been run continuously. The ads you see over and over again in magazines are probably the effective ones.

YELLOW PAGES

For many small woodshops, Yellow Pages ads are a necessary evil. Billed monthly, the cost of these ads could be high. However, for many general woodworking shops, the ads pay for themselves. To get the most out of your Yellow Pages advertising, you should try the following:

▶ Use your graphic designer and copywriter to create the ads. They'll be much more effective than the "free" layouts offered by the Yellow Pages.

▶ Negotiate mercilessly for the lowest possible rate, better placement, extra colors and larger size.

▶ If you've advertised in the Yellow Pages for years, use your seniority to demand better placement on the page. You want to be near the beginning of your category, on the outside of the page rather than buried in the binding, and preferably on the top right-hand side of the spread.

▶ Keep track of how your customers heard of you and track the kind of work generated by your Yellow Pages ads. My brother found that his display ad brought in a lot of requests for repair work, which was invariably too small to be profitable. He went to a bold-faced, listing-only ad because most of his work comes from mailings and referrals.

TRACKING YOUR ADS

It is essential to track the effectiveness of all your marketing. Simply ask new customers where they heard of you and record their responses. Over time you will see how ads build up your identity in the minds of the customers. You'll also get an idea of the effectiveness of your mailings, networking and sales efforts. All of these things work together to build awareness of your business, gradually forcing your company's name into the mind of a customer who is seeking woodworking services. Tracking will also indicate which ads are the least effective.

Advertising, particularly in national publications, is a very sophisticated process that requires a great commitment of time, money and learning through experience. The payback may not come for many months. However, advertising can be a very effective marketing tool for the larger woodshop or one that is very specialized.

▼ ▼ ▼

Using marketing to raise your prices

Pricing your work

QUOTES AND ESTIMATES

One of the goals of your marketing plan has been to earn a good living as a woodworker. Besides bringing in work, you must also make sure that you are actually making money on the work you do. If you always give the lowest possible quote, you may always be busy, but you may not make money because you're paying yourself too little. Low-balling also means that you get a lot of work from bargain hunters, whose only concern is cost. These people will invariably expect the highest-quality work at the lowest possible cost and will often spend large amounts of your time complaining and avoiding payment.

When you make a really low bid, you may have to cut corners because you get in over your head or you run into problems you didn't anticipate (and didn't charge for). Once you've established a reputation for being cheap, you'll always be expected to be at rock bottom. And you may attract customers who have little respect for your abilities.

The primary reasons for underbidding a job are inexperience and fear. You're afraid that you'll lose a job you desperately need. The irony is that many people soliciting bids automatically throw out the high and low bids, figuring that they represent either inexperience or greed. If the situation requires a low bid (as in certain government bidding where they must, by law, choose the low bid), you should be very careful not to overlook any potential problems that could put you in the red.

▼▼▼

USING MARKETING TO RAISE YOUR PRICES

When you have a reputation as a professional who does the job right the first time and is finished on schedule, you will not have to be the low bidder. Your reputation will precede you, paving the way for a reasonable quote with a good profit. I can't say how many times people have been surprised when they found that a truly top-of-the-line company was able to match prices with some of their lesser-known competitors. Because careful reputation building had raised expectations, they were able to blow away the competition at their own price. When making a bid on a job, there are guidelines you should follow when preparing the quote.

▶ Meet with the buyer, the designers and anyone else with decision-making power and gather as much information as possible. Make a list of problems that could crop up. These include money, financing, time and scheduling, coordination with other aspects of the project, taste, design, resource availability, emotional attachments and politics. Try to address all of these problems in your quote and presentation.

▶ Send your information packet (brochure, introductory letter, recent projects list) to all interested parties, even if you already have. Tell potential customers in your letter that you are preparing a bid for them and want to familiarize them with you and your business. By doing so, you are establishing your track record and showing a thorough approach. I guarantee that very few of your competitors will take this step. I know a company that did a lot of blind bidding for work at colleges and sent company information to all of the purchasing people at each bid site. The company gained an edge because each purchaser had heard of the company already. And the strategy worked.

▶ Use letterhead or a quote form for your quote. It should show your logo and business name in a professional manner. Computers have made it possible for tiny businesses to have the appearance of larger ones. Amateurish, handwritten bids are not acceptable. Your clearly written, easy-to-read bid will stand out to the weary person sorting through complex, bewildering piles of quotes.

- Cover all the issues in a succinct fashion. Make sure you've addressed the questions of who, when, why, where and how before you say how much.

- If drawings are unclear, or if they specify unusual materials or construction details, call and ask for clarification. Remember, a brief, professional-to-professional conversation means the customer has invested a little more time in you. Don't throw that investment away by asking dumb questions, wasting time or being unprepared when you call.

- Include a cover letter with the quote. In the letter, address the less tangible issues like taste and style and reinforce any points you consider important about your bid. For instance, if you are including installation as part of the bid, emphasize your experience in this area and explain how the client can save time and money by having you install the work. The letter is a final sales pitch. Last but not least, thank the customer for considering your company and say you look forward to doing the work.

- Follow up your bid with a phone call, checking to see if any aspect of the bid requires clarification.

- Last but not least, respond to all requests for bids or quotes immediately! I've found that fast, accurate response is perhaps the single, most effective action you can take to secure the value of your bid in the customer's eyes. We are all used to people saying they will do something and then failing to do it, so prompt action and interested attention to details will make you stand out. Do the bid today and fax or mail it this afternoon, if possible.

Professionalism impresses people, especially when it comes from crafts-people who work with their hands. Unfortunately, we live in a society that does not always respect the value of hands-on skills. But you can change this perception and meet the so-called "professionals" who need your abilities by acting in a way they are familiar with. Your professional approach says that you are on their wavelength and understand their problems, which helps you achieve the rapport that is critical to closing the sale.

PRICING YOUR WORK

Pricing has always been a marketing decision. Your prices are not based on your needs but on the price the market will bear. We follow the capitalistic law of supply and demand. I remember a spirited debate in the letters section of a woodworking publication about how to price work. It was apparent to me that many of the woodworkers writing the letters did not understand the nature of a capitalist marketplace. One writer said he decided what tool he needed to buy that month and priced his work accordingly. Another offered a formula where he summed up the cost of his materials and then added on a percentage for his labor. I wondered how he would have priced something that was extremely labor-intensive but required a few dollar's worth of materials, like a chair. Other readers discussed retrieving materials from old buildings to cut costs without taking into consideration the value of their time. All of these ideas, however well-intentioned, do not consider the primary determiner of price: the customer.

No matter how you price your work, it is vital to put a value on all of your time and to make a profit. Here's a simple formula you can use to price your work so that you can give a fairly accurate quote:

price = labor + materials + overhead + profit.

Put a value on your time. Find out how much someone else would pay you to do the work, on an hourly basis. It may be $13 per hour. Adjust that figure for any special knowledge or abilities you may have, which might bring your hourly price up to $15. This is your salary. Go over the job specifications and add up how many hours you'll spend on the job, including running errands, ordering supplies, talking on the phone and going to meetings. If you have helpers or partners, figure their time at the applicable rate. Multiply the hours by the rates to get a labor figure and add on a small percentage, say 10%, for errors in your estimates. If the job is small and will take you about 40 hours, you will reach a figure of around $660 (40 x $15 = $600; 10% x $600 = $60).

Now add up all the material costs involved, including finishing materials, wood, hardware, sandpaper and glue. Let's say your materials cost is $150. Add that to the $660, and you're up to $810. Now you have to consider overhead. How much does it cost to keep your shop going over a year? Consider rent, utilities, phone, marketing costs, insurance, tools that have a short life and office supplies. (Work up this figure before you start any estimates.) Let's say your yearly overhead is $18,000. This comes out to about $350 per week. Because the job will take one week, add the $350 to your number and get $1,160. But you're not out of the woods yet. Now you have to make some profit.

Profit helps your business grow, pays for tools, gets saved for retirement or other long-term goals or simply goes into your pocket at the end of the year. Without profit, you won't get ahead and will be unable to put aside funds for emergencies or other needs. In this example, add 15% for profit, or $174 (15% x $1,160), making the grand total $1,334.

Does this number look realistic when you consider what your competition is dealing with? Did you figure your salary too high or too low? If you pay yourself $5 an hour more than anyone else in your area, you may not be able to compete with other shops. Is your overhead extremely low or high? What do you know about your customer's budget? Maybe there is room for you to add a little more profit. Maybe your overhead is higher than average, and you must trim a little to compete with other woodworkers bidding on the job. This is where experience comes in. Resist the temptation to chop something off this price automatically. I recommend that you stick to your prices so long as they are realistic.

The example I'm using can give some other information about your business. Subtract the cost for materials ($1,334 - $150= $1,184), divide that number by the hours (40) to get $30 (approximate), which can be your hourly shop rate. This figure is valuable when you're asked to estimate small jobs, like repairs that don't have high material costs. I recommend sticking to a minimum shop rate of two hours or more for any job. My brother charges a minimum of four hours, figuring that nearly any job will tie up half a day; this practice also eliminates small jobs that take more time than they are worth. It's your call. You can always do small jobs when work is slow or do them in trade for other people's services.

This method of pricing works well on most jobs. But you will have to adapt for jobs where you are asked to give a piece rate on a quantity of work. This kind of estimate is dangerous if you don't get enough pieces to bring your costs down. If you are pricing a quantity of items, always use a sliding scale based on quantity, with the per-piece price dropping as the quantity rises. (For more information on money management or pricing, consult your accountant.)

BECOMING A LOCAL EXPERT

This chapter is about publicity. It is titled "Becoming a Local Expert" because that should be one of the goals of your publicity campaign. First, a definition of the word "local." If you work primarily in one geographic area, local means what it says: nearby. If you work within a specialized niche, serving restaurant designers, for instance, the area you want to become better known in is not defined geographically. It is a specialized community defined by interest, which is called your locality.

Once you know your locality, you can set about building a reputation as the woodworking expert in that locality. Once you've achieved this recognition, you'll be called upon for your expert opinion, mentioned and interviewed and, most important, referred to when someone has a question about woodworking. Becoming a local expert can be accomplished by using a very powerful and relatively inexpensive marketing tool: publicity.

WHAT IS PUBLICITY?

Publicity and public relations are marketing tactics used to build your identity in the marketplace. Publicity can be used to promote a new business or product, to develop an artistic reputation or to make you famous (if that's your objective). A favorable mention in the media makes a much stronger impression than a similar amount of paid advertising because the media are widely perceived to be less biased, telling stories only for the interest of their audiences.

Your publicity can take many forms. The most basic include new business announcements, gallery-opening announcements and the occasional quote in the news. Eventually you'll write articles and give interviews, you'll get reviews of your work, you'll possibly be the subject of a human-interest story on the news, or you may write a regular column in a trade magazine. You may eventually write books on woodworking, give workshops and become a well-known expert. All of these things come about, in part, because of publicity. You are marketing yourself and your skills to the media as something that will interest readers, listeners or viewers. You must catch the attention of editors who are deluged with boring press releases from people who are out to get free advertising. It is important to remember that the media are on a never-ending quest for interesting material to put between the ads that pay the bills. Package your publicity right, and you'll get some coverage.

ORGANIZING YOUR PUBLICITY

One of the first things that Chris and Max thought of doing when they formed Arcadia Woodworks was sending out announcements about their new business to the local press. It was a good idea, but I suggested that they plan a simple campaign of contacts to build awareness of Arcadia Woodworks gradually within the local media community. I recommended the following steps, which should work for your business, too:

► Assemble a media list.

► Look for opportunities to tell your story.

► Prepare your press release.

► Follow up.

▶ Generate more coverage.

▶ Develop a fact card.

Your media list should include local newspapers, business and general-interest magazines, radio stations, TV stations, local associations, like the local chapters of the AIA and ASID, and the local builder's association. The media list should be constantly expanding and should include addresses, fax and phone numbers and, most important, up-to-date names of contacts. Rather than just sending your materials to "the editor" or "the features editor," call and ask who would handle a story like yours. Names are important, and be sure to double-check the spelling.

A comprehensive media list for a woodshop would probably have only 20 to 30 names on it. However, by establishing yourself with those 20 to 30 people, you can generate considerable free publicity for your business.

If you've built a line of unusual children's furniture that you'll be bringing to a local craft fair, a press release sent to all the local media might get you a spot on the news or a color photo in the features section of a local paper. If you've recently been contracted to build a corporate library for a growing local company, send the story out to all the business editors in town. You might become a resource that editors call to ask about similar projects. It's important to tell your story. If your work features the many new water-based finishes, the angle may be the environmental aspects and safety issues involved. The story might be about a line of furnishings that is nontoxic to children and is part of the general move away from petrochemicals. How many parents will turn to the woodworker who is a specialist in safe finishes? Every woodworker in your state may use these finishes, but you may be the first to tell the story. I can see the headline and the subhead of the newspaper article:

ARCADIA WOODWORKS SWITCHES TO ENVIRONMENTALLY SAFE FINISHES

Owner Chris Zyslinski praises quality
of the new low-impact, nontoxic finishes

A press release is a standard format for releasing information for publication. You should learn how to write a press release, or find a writer who can tell your story. You can simply type it on your letterhead. At the top left-hand side of the page, type FOR IMMEDIATE RELEASE; beneath that, put the date and your name and phone number. Skip a few spaces and write your headline. It should be as catchy as you can make it. The ideal headline addresses the who, what, why, when and how of your story. In your first paragraph, tell the whole story as concisely as possible. The next few paragraphs should elaborate, using real people's names and examples to enliven the story. Avoid flowery language and overuse of adjectives and "creative" writing. Editors will lose interest as soon as the fluff starts flowing. Finish up with a paragraph that tells the relevant facts once more and asks contacts to call you for more information. Go down a few more spaces and type the number 33, which is a newspaper technique of indicating that the end of the story has been reached. Try to stick to one page, double spaced, with wide margins (an example is on the facing page).

If you hire a writer to do your press release, read it critically. Be careful not to omit important information, misspell names or quote people without their permission. Include pictures and hand-write a brief note to the editor, saying thank you for taking the time to read your release. Be sure to tell the editor to call you personally, anytime, if there are any questions. After a week or two, call and ask if the editor has received your release. If the answer is yes, ask if there are any questions. Editors are very busy, so keep your conversation brief unless the editor keeps it going. Offer additional photos or more information.

Use your coverage to generate more coverage. Make copies of any articles printed about your business or highlight quotes from any broadcast and send it out with a press release to other media. If you have articles published either by or about you, send copies to all of your customers. Most national magazines and some local ones can sell you full-color reprints of articles. They may even be able to add some copy, turning the article into an effective marketing piece. Otherwise, just send out photocopies.

Keep a file of press clippings and assemble the best quotes and coverage into a sampler on one or two pages. This not only becomes a part of your portfolio but will also be effective when dealing with gallery owners or finagling a good spot at a large show. Fame has its advantages, and a few press clippings show that you've got a reputation.

If you write articles or sell plans for woodworking magazines, your previous press coverage may help you convince an editor that you are an expert in your field. Even a local clipping gives you a big advantage over the amateurish efforts that many unfortunate editors wade through daily.

Send your media list a simple fact card about your business. A fact card can generate calls from the media that establish you as a local expert. You simply put together a rotary card file card with the heading "Woodworking" on the top tab. Under that heading list your company name, tagline and all the contact information, including name(s) and phone number(s). Put a brief note in with the card, explaining that you would be happy to help out if the contact ever needs any information on woodworking (or any particular specialty you might have). Many editors and writers keep a resource file of contacts they have made over the years. When they need a story on kitchen cabinetry or restoring old furniture, they'll thumb through and find your card.

FOR IMMEDIATE RELEASE

Date: September 12, 1995
Contact: Max Gert (777-777-7777)

Local Artist Revives Grandmother Clocks as Functional Sculpture

Woodworker and artisan Max Gert will show his series of Next-Generation Grandmother Clocks at a gala reception in The Atrium Gallery on Saturday, October 1, 1995. The six mantel-size clocks feature unique aniline-dye finishes and jewelry-quality metal ornamentation. The clock style is based on the Arts and Crafts movement while incorporating modernist design elements. A limited edition of 10 sets are being made to order.

"In designing and fabricating this set, I sought to revive the idea of a studio as design atelier," says Gert. "My partner, Chris Zyslinski, and I hope to see our shop, Arcadia Woodworks, develop a reputation as a center of fine woodworking craft and design. This series was conceived as the first products of our fine-arts studio. We still continue to do business as a high-quality woodshop and feel that this kind of work is an excellent complement to that part of our business."

The clocks feature hidden doors, mechanical works and fit well with a contemporary interior. The grandmother clock is smaller than the grandfather clocks we are familiar with. The smaller scale allowed the artist to build a series that is both functional and beautiful.

The show at The Atrium Gallery starts with an opening reception on Saturday evening at 7 p.m. The show will continue through November 15 and is open to the public. For more information, call Marcia Smith at The Atrium Gallery (777-666-6666) or Max Gert or Chris Zyslinski at Arcadia Woodworks (777-777-7777). The Atrium Gallery is located at 495 Main St.

-33-

Cards that fit the standard-size card files are available in punch-out form on 8½ x 11 sheets. Make up a master and make enough copies to enclose them with any media mailings you do. You may want to have a set professionally typeset by your graphic designer to send to customers. It is an inexpensive way to keep your name at your customer's fingertips.

▼▼▼

WRITING ARTICLES AND BOOKS

There are thousands of hobbyist woodworkers who are starved for professional tips and guidance. Many books and magazine articles are published by woodworkers like you. Some of these writers eventually become known as experts among their peers and even make a little extra money showing others how to do things. If you are interested in writing, photography or teaching, or have a specialized knowledge to pass on, you can probably get published. There are a few simple guidelines to follow.

Pick the publication you think is best suited for your article idea. If you have a step-by-step plan for building a Shaker-style cabinet, then a hobbyist magazine that features similar articles would be a good choice. An article explaining a complex router technique might be better suited for magazines catering to professional and highly skilled craftspeople. A story about your business would be aimed at a trade paper. Remember targeting? It is the key to marketing your story as well as your business. Pick the right publication and then read back issues to get a feel for the publication's style. It is a good idea to ask for writer's guidelines, which will help you format your story in a way that is acceptable to the editors.

Once you have an idea and have chosen a magazine in which you'd like to publish it, write a letter that pitches your idea to the magazine editor. Tell the editor who would be interested in the article and why. Describe your qualifications and include an outline of the article. If a plan is involved or if you have photos, include them. Send the letter, the outline, the photos and a self-addressed stamped envelope (SASE) for a reply. You don't have to write the article yet. Wait until you get a firm commitment from the editor. The editor may suggest a different approach or ask for more information. If you get rejected, try another magazine or market. Many magazines understand that woodworkers may not be great writers and will take your ideas and polish them up for you, if the ideas are good.

If writing interests you, there are many books in the reference section of your library on how to write and submit articles for publication. The techniques they teach will really make a difference in how an editor reacts to your work. Successful articles can lead to books, which can really broaden your reputation as a woodworker. It's not a bad way to build your business, either. If you can't write, team up with someone who can.

GALLERIES AND SHOWS

Participating in a group show at a local gallery is an excellent way to get publicity. Keep tabs on which galleries in your region feature crafts and make sure the curators know who you are and what you do. You should seek gallery attention at all the possible galleries within a day's drive of your shop. Make appointments to show the gallery owners or curators your work and ask to be put on their mailing lists. Join every local arts association. Go to openings and schmooze with others, talk to other artists and get to know the art crowd. If you make a connection, give an invitation to your shop (studio) to see your work. Eventually, you'll get asked to join a group show or participate in a thematic show. Be sure to enter slides of your best work in any and all juried shows. Watch the arts magazines for announcements and respond as often as possible.

If a gallery owner responds favorably to your work, you may be able to arrange a show, either alone or with another woodworker or artist/craftsperson. Draw up your own marketing plan for publicizing your show and brainstorm with the gallery owner. Be sure to send announcements and invitations to the opening to each person on your mailing lists. Give a great party at the opening, and you'll have an ideal networking opportunity on your hands. If you do custom woodworking in addition to your own designs, bring a pile of brochures to distribute to attendees.

If you own a more commercial woodshop, you might consider participating in trade shows and home shows that highlight your company's abilities. Treat these sales opportunities the same as a gallery opening and send out free passes to customers. And don't forget the press release.

Publicity is an inexpensive and effective tool for marketing your business. It can also be very satisfying when you and your work receive public recognition. Because you labor in a shop on your own much of the time, you may often feel that you are not making an impact with your work. There's nothing wrong with tooting your own horn when you've done something you are proud of. If your story is interesting, it will get told. You just have to shepherd it along and be available when the time is right.

▼ ▼ ▼

Contact, contact, contact

Referrals

Referral follow-up

THE IMPORTANCE OF REGULAR CONTACT AND FOLLOW-UP

Customer satisfaction is the key to the long-term success of your wood-working business. It has been estimated that a satisfied customer will tell one to three other people about a good experience while an unsatisfied customer will tell eight to 10 people about a bad experience. Because one of the primary goals of your marketing efforts is to get referrals, it should be obvious that keeping your customers happy is vital. Happy customers will send you work. But even more important, unhappy customers will bad-mouth you, destroying your reputation (and your livelihood.)

You must ensure a consistently high level of quality in everything you do. The first time you skimp or cut corners on a piece of work, you are headed down a dangerous path. Inevitably, that piece of work will be the one seen by a potential customer, or its owner will tell the world how he has been cheated. Learning the woodworking skills necessary to maintain consistently high quality is not what this book is about. However, maintaining a consistent quality of customer service and follow-up is very important to marketing your business successfully. You should pursue excellence as a regular part of running your business. To ensure excellent service, plan for regular contact and follow-up during and after a project.

CONTACT, CONTACT, CONTACT

You've heard it over and over again in the pages of this book. You must keep the lines of communication open with your customers. Memories are short, and it is often a long stretch from one job for a customer to the time the next one is being planned. If you don't stay in touch, the customer may not think of you when asked for a referral or when planning another project. Regular contact also gives you many opportunities to offer valuable advice and to make sure your customers know about all the services you offer. The customer who commissions you to build a child's bed may not realize that you can build cabinetry for his office or for a kitchen the customer and wife are planning with their designer. But you can tell them about your other skills by sending them postcards, brochures and informative articles on a regular basis.

Marketing is a numbers game. You determine how many customers you must reach to generate enough work to be profitable. You seek certain customer profiles and get demographics together that tell you how many of these highly targeted customers there are. Then you make contact with these customers on a regular basis, gradually building awareness of you and your business until the customers are ready to buy. Then, once they have become satisfied customers, you use regular follow-up to enlist them as informal salespeople for your business. Each of these activities includes a number of contacts that build a personal and professional relationship over time. Ideally, the result is a customer who takes an active interest in the success of you and your business.

Let's take a look at how Max and Chris maintained contact with a customer over time. Chris made a checklist form to record contacts with a customer. He and Max kept this contact checklist in the customer's file and used it as a general record of telephone conversations, mailings and any unusual or relevant events or requests that came up. This way, either Chris or Max could pull out the contact checklist when they got a call and would have a brief history of their experience with that customer at hand. If they had a computer-software package for customer contact, they would have kept this information in a database, constantly upgrading it and providing signals to remind them to mail a card or make a follow-up call. Because they had not yet put all of their information on a computer, they kept notes on their wall calendar to remind them of these marketing milestones (for more about using calendars, see p. 147).

CONTACT CHECKLIST

Initial contacts:

☐ Mail brochure.

☐ Make cold call to set up appointment.

☐ Mail postcard.

☐ Mail second brochure after six months.

Total contacts: **4**

Contacts with interested prospects:

☐ Make appointment to show portfolio.

☐ Request to bid on work.

☐ Meet or call to discuss bid.

☐ Send out bid with marketing materials enclosed.

☐ Make follow-up call to answer any questions.

☐ Send copy of informative article about kitchen design, characteristics of various woods or the like (relevant to project).

Total contacts: **6**

Contact during project:

☐ Set up meetings for planning (2).

☐ Discuss drawings on phone.

☐ Send samples of finish or materials.

☐ Get approval to build.

☐ Install or deliver completed project.

Total contacts: **5**

Contacts after project completion:

☐ Call after one week to check for satisfaction.

☐ Send a thank-you note.

☐ Send postcard (if the card shows the customer's project, send a pile with stamps attached so that customer can send copies to friends or colleagues).

☐ Call again after three months to check satisfaction and to ask for referrals.

☐ Send copies of articles by or about you, and send updated projects list or new brochures or postcards.

☐ Send a holiday card.

Total contacts: **6**

Total contacts for one year: 21

If 21 contacts seems like a lot, remember that many are brief phone calls and pieces of mail sent out as part of your business, such as quotes and invoices. Even a simple marketing plan can generate many contacts. The important thing is to recognize that even small contacts keep your customer aware of you and your business. By thinking of these contacts as part of your overall marketing strategy, you will get into the habit of asking for referrals and following up on leads that can bring in work. If your customer list has only 100 names on it, and you make an average of 10 contacts with each prospect over a year's time, you've made contact 1,000 times. That's 1,000 opportunities to generate business. Learn your sales skills, and you will convert enough of those opportunities into work to keep yourself busy and prosperous. Ignore the opportunity, and you'll sit in the shop wondering where the work is.

REFERRALS

Referrals are the ultimate source of business for any woodworker. I can't tell you how many times I've asked woodworkers or other small business-people what their principal marketing method is, and they've answered "word of mouth." These people inevitably complain about not having enough business. It is important to understand that word of mouth is a marketing tool that you can use to generate business. The key to generating good word of mouth is to ask for referrals from satisfied customers. Word of mouth is also the result of every marketing tool you utilize—if each tool is used effectively. Ads generate word of mouth, publicity generates it, then brochures and phone calls keep it going. You can magnify the effectiveness of these tools by asking for referrals from satisfied customers on a regular basis.

If asking customers to send you business seems terribly self-serving, keep this in mind: People love to give friends and business acquaintances referrals to good resources like you. When they can recommend a good woodworker to a friend, they become a valuable resource in that friend's eyes. Part of this is because we all like to be well connected. When you ask for referrals from your customers, you are asking them to participate in the success of your business.

I have to note that asking for referrals means you are accepting a great responsibility. You cannot disappoint the valued customer who went out on a limb for you. Every job that comes from a referral should be treated as an incredibly valuable favor. Both your reputation and your customer's reputation are on the line.

If you ask for referrals, you must also make them. You've asked for loyalty from your customers, so you must reciprocate by sending them business, helping them save money, hooking them up with resources, such as other tradespeople or suppliers. Each of these favors you do will result in a big payback. As a small businessperson, you know how much it means when someone sends you work or helps you when you are in a bind. Look for ways to return that favor. Remember, what goes around comes around.

REFERRAL FOLLOW-UP

When you get a referral from a customer, a supplier, a friend or an acquaintance, be sure that you thank that person for the reference in writing. I have found it is more than worth it to send out a small gift with a thank-you note. These little tokens really mean a lot to the person who receives them. It's just one more way of building a close relationship with your customers.

On the opposite side of the transaction, when you make a referral, it is in your interest to make sure that the recipient of the referral knows where it came from. After you make a referral, call the person and say you've referred him to so-and-so, then give him a little background about the customer. In my business, when I get a referral like this, I'll usually send a brochure, with a note saying that so-and-so mentioned that the customer needed some help. By taking the first step, you can make it easy for a customer to work with you. I've turned many referrals into business by simply offering my services, sending out some useful information and following up. I do this all after I learn that my name was given out but before the customer can contact me.

ARCADIA
WORKS
A REFERRAL

▼ ▼ ▼

Chris got a call from his attorney, John, who told him that he had just given Chris' name to Fred Johnson. Fred needed a custom desk that could handle several computer monitors for his investment business. It needed to look like fine furniture while functioning like an office cube. John said that Fred told him he'd been looking for a factory-made desk but couldn't find one that worked. He was willing to spend a certain amount of money to get what he needed but was nervous about hiring a woodworker to build his desk because he didn't know how long it would take or if the piece would look strange or cost a fortune. Armed with the information that John had given him, Chris found an article on some

of the new computer furniture that was becoming available, and he photocopied it. He wrote a note saying that he could use the commercial computer desk as a base and adapt it to match Fred's needs while retaining the use of its special design characteristics. The combination would save money and do the job. Plus, it wouldn't take as long as building from scratch. Chris faxed the article and the letter to Fred and followed up with a mail package that contained the same information and a brochure. The next day, he called Fred to introduce himself and ask if he'd received the materials. Fred took the call and was very grateful for Chris' help. And Arcadia got the job.

That wasn't the end of it, though. To say thanks for the referral, Chris and Max sent John a set of bookends they'd designed and made a small production run of the design. John was thrilled and has made referrals on a regular basis since. Fred can't say enough good things about Arcadia Woodworks, and he mentions the company every time a client of his admires the desk. He even asked for a stack of Arcadia's brochures to pass out. And to keep the circle going, Max and Chris have sent several of their friends who own small businesses to John's law firm.

CHAPTER 21

PROFIT CENTERS

▼ ▼ ▼

Products

Services

If you are a general woodworker whose work varies from project to project, there are probably slow times when work and money are not coming in. A slow period is the time to develop new products and services you can market. I call these products and services profit centers. Profit centers often start out as things you do on the side while pursuing your main business as a custom woodshop. Sometimes a profit center turns out to be lucrative enough to become your main business, to become an entirely new business or to contribute significantly to your cash flow. If you are not as busy as you want or would like a change, think about adding one or more profit centers to your business.

In this chapter, I'm going to show you some potential profit centers and how to market them. Ideas for new products or services may be in front of you all the time. You simply need to find a way to gain from them. First let's take a look at products.

PRODUCTS

A product is something that you make to sell. A woodworker who sells at craft fairs or shops often has developed a product line. The product line is normally a group of related items that are stylistically similar and can be produced in quantities large enough to bring the individual prices down to a competitive level. Let's say your small shop designs and builds a line of wooden furnishings for toddlers. The line could include a rocking chair, an adjustable height-stick that attaches to the wall and measures the toddler's growth, a toy chest or a desk. The pieces feature bright-colored nontoxic finishes, rounded edges and corners and a unique, bright design and look. During slow periods you'll set up jigs and build 20 to 30 of each piece in an assembly line fashion. You have a flyer featuring color photos of the whole line in a child's room that emphasizes the style, safety features and colorful appeal of the products. You send out the flyer to children's shops and sell the products at craft fairs during summer weekends. Over the slower winter months, you may build 100 to 200 pieces and keep them in a rental storage space, sending them out to shops to fill orders and then loading them into a rented van to display at shows. With the markup at shows, you may make an average of $20 per piece on the show sales, generating an extra $2,000 to $4,000 in income from your slow periods.

In this example, you could continue at that level and make a good part of your income from your products. Or you could take it a step further, either hiring help to build the pieces and doing more marketing, or licensing the designs to a manufacturer of children's furnishings and collecting royalties. It's not easy, but it's possible. Other ideas include:

▶ Selling project plans to other woodworkers.

▶ Selling specialized jigs or tools of your design.

▶ Writing books or how-to pamphlets on areas you specialize in.

▶ Building furniture prototypes for manufacturers.

▶ Developing special products like custom mixed finishes or hardware.

▶ Finding specialized niche markets and serving them as an expert resource.

▶ Producing kits or blanks for specialized hobbyists, which may include duck decoys, gun stocks, musical-instrument parts and canvas stretchers for artists.

▶ Building commercial products, such as retail store fixtures, bars, bookshelves for law libraries and computer furniture.

Niches are often found after you are asked to do an unusual piece or project and then you realize that there are other customers with a need for similar specialized items. Try to spot these opportunities and do the research necessary to find out if they can be profitable. Any of these product examples could be marketed through classified ads in magazines that cater to hobbyists, artists and model makers. The work may not be particularly exciting, but it can become a profitable sideline.

Product ideas are generated by demand rather than by imagination. When you see an opportunity or have an idea for a potential product, spend your energy doing a little basic market research before you build prototypes or commit to ads or tooling. The research techniques I discussed in Chapter 6 will also be useful here.

SERVICES

Selling products is not the only way to maintain your business during slow periods. Woodworking is a service business, too. You provide a number of services, including planning, design, supplying resources like hardware, installation and advice. Each of these services is an opportunity to create a profit center. For example, if you are a cabinetmaker with extensive experience building and installing kitchens, you might consider going into the kitchen-design business as a sideline. Your knowledge of what makes a functional and attractive workspace is a salable skill. Other possible service spin-offs include:

▶ Doing custom finishing, including faux finishes, spraying, dyes and stains.

▶ Specializing in an aspect of woodworking that you can sell to other woodshops, such as turning, carving, veneering, lamination or wood bending.

▶ Specializing in historical design, renovation and reproduction.

▶ Working as a consultant.

The key to consulting is effective use of resources. For example, if you have extensive experience with commercial woodwork, you might provide expertise to an architecture or building firm that designs large jobs, such as hotels or hospitals. To these firms, you are a skilled outside expert who can help keep costs down and quality up. Consulting can be lucrative, but it is often difficult to break in to the field before you have a reputation. Many of the publicity tools in Chapter 19 can help you spread your reputation so that you can eventually become a consultant. If it is cost effective for a company to hire your expertise for a few days, you can charge a good rate for your time. Consulting fees range from $250 to $1,000 per day, so you can see why it might be worth pursuing.

Profit centers are often found while pursuing your regular daily business. A need presents itself or someone asks you if you can provide a service you've never thought about before. The key is to look for these profit opportunities and then determine if they can be profitable and interesting. If someone wants you to build 100 wooden widgets, and you've got the time, why not? Or if a customer asks you to look over a group of bids, charge a consulting fee. Your abilities and expertise are valuable for more than working in the shop.

ARCADIA'S FIRST PROFIT CENTER

▼ ▼ ▼

Max's line of grandmother clocks is a great example of building a product line without becoming a factory. He had spent his slow times over the first year of Arcadia's existence designing a half-dozen clocks and building a prototype of each. They were beautifully designed, a nice size for a home, and the level of craftsmanship approached fine art. The prices were steep, and they really needed to be marketed through a respected gallery to reach his targeted audience of affluent collectors.

First the clocks were photographed in color to highlight the dyes and the interesting wood selection. Each clock was given a name, and the fact that they were next-generation grandmother clocks was emphasized in the press release (see p. 131). A color postcard was prepared, and Max began meeting with the owners of several galleries. He also entered one of the clocks in a local juried show and won in the woodworking division, an achievement that netted a corporate sale and a photo in the local paper. As a result, a prestigious gallery in a nearby major city took on the line and planned a show with two other woodworkers. The clocks were marketed as a line of six different designs in a limited edition of 10 each. The shop was also equipped to build custom clocks. It was hoped that collectors would be interested in purchasing an entire set. Max and the gallery owner worked together to get coverage in major craft and art magazines and over the first year sold a number of clocks. Chris and Max worked together on the clocks during slow periods and are planning a new series to be marketed as products of the Arcadia Design Atelier. They hoped to build a recognizable style that would interest collectors and gradually build a market for all of their work. If it worked out, they would be able to spend more time on their own designs and less on the commercial jobs that were paying their bills.

Max's clocks were a long-term project. They did not even generate any real profits right away. The goal was to free Arcadia from its dependence on commercial work, which was uneven. Both Chris and Max were beginning to realize that this project could lead them into unexpected territory. A major clock manufacturer had contacted them with an interest in the designs. A few months previously, they would have had a hard time dealing with such major changes in their business. But because their marketing savvy was growing by leaps and bounds, they were ready for whatever would happen.

MAKING TIME FOR MARKETING

How does anyone find the time to do all of this stuff? When you're backed up with two or three jobs, it seems impossible to put aside time for marketing. The sad thing is that those busy times are when it is most important to continue the marketing efforts you started when things were slow. This is because you are always marketing to build future business. If you slack off now, you may not have any work six months from now. You must find a way to keep on track with your marketing efforts day in and day out. The most important way is to develop good time-management skills.

▼ ▼ ▼

TIME MANAGEMENT

To make the most effective use of your time for marketing, you must develop three special time-management skills: planning, prioritizing and using people as resources. Planning consists of putting together a simple marketing plan with a calendar of regular activities so that you'll always know how much time to put aside for marketing each day, week and month. Prioritizing determines which activities are most important so that you can spend your most productive time and energy on those activities. The third way to manage your time effectively is to use people as resources. The only way to give yourself more than your allotted 24 hours in a day is to share your tasks with others. In this chapter I'll show you some of the ways you can use planning, prioritizing and people to help you stay on track with your marketing.

PLANNING

In the first part of this book, I walked you through the process of researching and creating a marketing plan. One of the most important aspects of that plan is a calendar of marketing activities (see p. 60) that you can follow daily to ensure that you get everything done most effectively. The calendar also makes sure that you are consistent in your marketing approach to customers and that you follow up with them frequently.

Good time management will help your business. Buy a good daily planner, one that is in a binder and has an address section and a goals section. It should be expandable. There are several secrets to using a planner.

▶ Put all of your appointments, phone numbers, meetings, daily goals for mailings, calls and presentations and notes about your contacts in this planner.

▶ Always carry your planner with you and always use the same one. Don't scribble notes on a calendar at home and transfer them later. You'll forget or miss something. Keep everything in one book and use it as a journal, idea center, scheduling helper and contact list. By using the same planner, you'll always be able to check your progress, and you'll never forget an appointment, overbook yourself or be unprepared for a meeting.

▶ Start your day with a look through your planner. Keep it in front of you when you make calls and record your activities in each day's page. You'll soon see how to utilize your time more effectively.

Planners are great for day-to-day planning. But for long-term planning, I suggest you buy a large wall calendar that shows an entire year. This type of calendar is available at office-supply stores. When you get it, write down your entire year's marketing activities in the appropriate spots, including mailings, shows, conferences, meetings and classes. Mark important deadlines in red and block out time for upcoming work. Seeing everything on the wall will make it easier to understand where your time is going. You'll start to see relationships between different tactics, and you'll be able to head off potential conflicts before they become problems. And these planning tools will keep you on track with your marketing activities.

PRIORITIZING

Each of your activities has a priority attached to it. Unfortunately, when you don't know what those priorities are, you may spend too much time on low-priority items, which leaves little time for important ones. If you can assign a priority level to each of your activities, you'll find that more high-priority items will get done.

One easy way to determine the importance of an activity is to take a selfish approach. Look at your weekly to-do list. Rank the items according to which ones will benefit you the most. Remember, some of the least-pleasant activities may actually benefit you the most over time. For instance, if things are slowing, or if you have a month ahead with no work in sight, take a look at the marketing tasks that you have been avoiding. My guess is that you've skipped something important, like calling for appointments. This task may be your least favorite, but it will bring in work and get you started on meeting new customers face to face. By assigning a high priority to phone calls, you'll be more likely to do them.

Here's an exercise that can help you get to work on high-priority tasks. Pick one task and totally immerse yourself in it, doing it as well as possible and, at the same time, trying to find the very best, most efficient way to accomplish it. Give it the same energy and attention that you would invest in something you love to do. This ability to immerse oneself in necessary tasks is what often separates a very successful person from an unsuccessful one. Rather than avoiding or complaining, the successful person looks for the challenge in any task and does it as well as possible.

USING PEOPLE AS RESOURCES

Unless you live in a cave, you are probably dependent on interaction with others. Part of that interaction comes from the sharing of tasks, unique skills and abilities. As a woodworker, you are capable of accomplishing certain things that others don't have the time and/or the training to do themselves. As a result, it is worth their time to hire you to build things. They use you as a resource, and you in turn receive compensation. One of the easiest ways to find more time for marketing is to find people who can help you. You pay them for what they are good at and concentrate your efforts on what you are good at. As obvious as this seems, I've seen many small-business owners trying to save money by doing their own photos, graphic design and copywriting. The results are rarely successful and may, in fact, do some damage if they are amateurish. These people do not put a value on the expertise of others. As a result, a lot of valuable time and money is wasted.

The key is to view people as resources and use your address book or phone book as a resource bank. When you are putting together your marketing materials, enlist your resources and make them your allies. When you bring business to them, they have reason to take an active stake in your success. And when they have such a stake, you can trust them to do a good job, freeing you up to do what you do best.

HIRE A MARKETING DEPARTMENT

A lot of the day-to-day aspects of marketing are busy-work items, like mailings, scheduling meetings and writing letters. If you find yourself getting behind in these important tasks because you are busy running your business, consider hiring a "marketing department." I don't mean a roomful of people; I mean a part-time person to do some of the many tasks that keep your message going out to your customers. A marketing student from a local college or business school would probably jump at the chance to come in once or twice a week for a few hours and learn small-business marketing on the job. You might even be able to get someone as an intern for little or no money. You should look for enthusiasm, a good record at school and an outgoing personality. You'll want to teach the student as much about your business as possible and be available to answer questions. Make sure that he or she knows all of your marketing plans and strategies and try to get the person involved in the success of your business. You might even award a bonus when your combined efforts bring in a big job. And plan the workload so that the marketer will have plenty to do while at work.

Finding time for marketing is not impossible if you learn a few basic skills and take a long-term view of the things you are doing. Effective time management can mean the difference between spinning your wheels and being a successful woodworker. The most important thing you can do to succeed is to start your marketing now and never stop. It's not just a part of starting a business, it's an integral part of the day-to-day work of being in business. There are very few activities that will do more to ensure the success of your woodworking business. Isn't it worth the effort to make a profitable living doing what you do best? This book has given you the basic tools of marketing. As you become more skilled, you'll understand and use the many more sophisticated tools available to bring more customers into your shop. Until then, spending the time to assemble and master your marketing plan will be a challenge. Take that challenge and enjoy it. You'll never wonder where your next job will be coming from. Good luck!

RESOURCES

This section is a list of sources of information for the small-business owner. I suggest reading these materials to get a better understanding of marketing and how it can help your woodworking business. Even if you come away from a book or magazine with just one profitable idea, you have more than justified its price. If you're starting out, I strongly suggest contacting the Small Business Administration for information and guidance. Check your phone book under "Federal Government" to find the nearest office. The SBA has many useful, free publications, can offer excellent help with planning and financing and may hook you up with a Service Corps of Retired Executives (SCORE) mentor who can help you find your way through the ins and outs of business management.

BOOKS

Business Planning Guide, 6th Edition, by David H. Bangs, Jr., Upstart Publishing Co., Inc., Dover, N.H., 1992.

Market Planning Guide: Gaining and maintaining the competitive edge by David H. Bangs, Jr., Upstart Publishing Co., Inc., Dover, N.H., 1989.

Excellent guides to writing and using business plans and marketing plans. A business plan forces you to consider every aspect of a business and becomes a necessary document if you ever need bank financing.

Growing A Business by Paul Hawken, Simon & Schuster, New York, N.Y., 1988.

One of the best books for anyone starting a business. Entertaining and realistic. Highly recommended.

Guerrilla Marketing: How to make big profits in your small business by Jay Conrad Levinson, Houghton Mifflin Co. Boston, Mass., 1989.

Guerrilla Marketing Attack: New strategies, tactics and weapons for winning big profits by Jay Conrad Levinson, Houghton Mifflin Co., Boston, Mass., 1989.

Guerrilla Marketing Excellence: The 50 golden rules for small business success by Jay Conrad Levinson, Houghton Mifflin Co., Boston, Mass., 1993.

Guerrilla Marketing Weapons: 100 affordable marketing methods for maximizing profits from your small business by Jay Conrad Levinson, Houghton Mifflin Co., Boston, Mass., 1990.

Guerrilla Selling: Unconventional tactics for increasing your sales by Bill Gallagher, Houghton Mifflin Co., Boston, Mass., 1992.

These are the definitive general small-business marketing books. They are based on the premise that a small-business marketer can beat out competition big and small by being innovative. The books provide many examples of strategy and tactics.

Prescription for Advertising: A common-sense cure for business owners and managers by Edmund A. Bruneau, Boston Books, Spokane, Wash., 1986.

The book for the business owner considering the use of advertising to promote the business. Bruneau tells the reader how to deal with writers, artists, agencies and media in a down-to-earth, expert voice.

Small Time Operator: How to start your own small business, keep your books, pay your taxes and stay out of trouble, 12th Edition, by Bernard Kamaroff, Bell Springs, Laytonville, Calif., 1992.

Understanding cash flow, billing and profits is vital to making marketing decisions. Small Time Operator is a classic how-to book for small-business accounting. Use this book to learn how to talk to your accountant (and save money).

Working At Woodworking: How to organize your shop and your business by Jim Tolpin, The Taunton Press, Newtown, Conn., 1991.

A glimpse into the professional woodworking life written by a working woodworker.

MAGAZINES AND PERIODICALS

Architectural Record

This expensive, glossy magazine is worth picking up to catch a glimpse into the world of commercial and residential architecture. Not only will you pick up on trends, but you may also find names to market your woodworking services to.

Custom Woodworking Business

A glossy trade magazine aimed at small- and medium-sized shops.

Fine Woodworking and **Fine Homebuilding**

The magazines for skilled amateurs and professionals. As a pro, your work will often be integrated into new construction and renovation projects. For that reason, you can't afford not to read Fine Homebuilding along with Fine Woodworking.

Inc. Magazine

A source of useful tips and advice from your peers.

Woodshop News

A trade magazine for the small, professional woodworking business. Good for its profiles of other woodworkers, sources for supplies and informative articles about the business of woodworking.

Wood & Wood Products

The trade magazine for big manufacturers. It may be worth subscribing to for its annual supplier's resource guide, an excellent reference for finding anything from pulls to TV elevators to European cabinets. When your architect specifies something exotic or unique, this is the place to find it and look like a hero.

INDEX

EDITOR: THOMAS C. MCKENNA

DESIGNER/LAYOUT ARTIST: CATHERINE CASSIDY

TYPEFACE: GARAMOND

PAPER: MEAD PAPER, 70 LB., MOISTRITE MATTE WEB

PRINTER: QUEBECOR PRINTING/HAWKINS, NEW CANTON, TENNESSEE